The Reformation
and Liberation Theology

The Reformation
and
Liberation Theology

Insights for the Challenges
of Today

Richard Shaull

Westminster/John Knox Press
Louisville, Kentucky

Book design by Gene Harris

First edition

Published by Westminster/John Knox Press
Louisville, Kentucky

PRINTED IN THE UNITED STATES OF AMERICA

9   8   7   6   5   4   3   2   1

Library of Congress Cataloging-in-Publication Data

Shaull, Richard.
  The reformation and liberation theology : insights for the challenges of today / Richard Shaull. — 1st ed.
      p.   cm.
  Includes bibliographical references.
  ISBN 0-664-25222-2

  1. Liberation theology.   2. Reformation.   3. Theology, Doctrinal—History—16th century.   4. Protestantism.   I. Title
BT83.57.S57   1991
270'.6—dc20   91-4519

To

Josef Hromadka

and

Paul Lehmann

who introduced me to the riches

of the Reformation heritage

and demonstrated its power

to transform life today.

Contents

The Reformation
and Liberation Theology

Preface

This book is the result of my rediscovery of the Protestant Reformation of the sixteenth century after I became involved in a New Reformation taking place today.

As someone brought up as a staunch Calvinist and trained theologically in the thought of Martin Luther, John Calvin, and their modern interpreters, the heritage of that earlier Reformation set the terms for my thought and my life. It captivated my conscience and awakened in me a yearning for the transformation of the world and for the radical renewal of the church as the instrument of God's redemptive work in history. But, over the years, I was forced to conclude that the church that had given me this vision seemed incapable of living by it.

A few years ago, however, my contact with Christian base communities and the theology of liberation in Latin America convinced me that a New Reformation had already begun. And as I participated in it, I found myself turning more and more to the Protestant Reformation and engaging in a new dialogue with it. I came to realize that this powerful spiritual movement was the major liberation movement in both church and society in sixteenth-century Europe. As I approached it once again with the questions being raised by Christians involved in liberation struggles today, I found myself discovering and appropriating more of its spiritual and theological riches.

I had a new sense of what the Reformation can contribute
to the renewal of the church and to the transformation of
society today. I found that the heritage by which I have
lived was being renewed and transformed, thus providing
greater resources for my dialogue with the theology of
liberation. And I began to imagine what an ongoing
dialogue between Reformation heritage and the work of
the Holy Spirit in today's New Reformation might contribute to those churches born of that earlier movement of
the Spirit, churches in the Reformed tradition.

This interaction has already begun, especially among
third-world Christians. The Departamento Ecuménico de
Investigaciones, an ecumenical study center in San José,
Costa Rica, has taken the initiative in bringing together
groups of Latin American pastors and laypersons, to study
their particular confessional heritages in the light of the
liberation struggle and liberation theology. In the 1990
Warfield Lectures at Princeton Theological Seminary,
entitled *Liberating Reformed Theology,* John de Gruchy, a
South African Calvinist scholar, examines the theology of
John Calvin in the light of the liberation struggle in South
Africa and Latin American liberation theology; he shows
how Reformed theology can not only be liberated in this
encounter but can also contribute significantly to liberation today. And Daniel Schipani, a Christian educator
from Argentina now teaching at the Associated Mennonite Biblical Seminaries in Elkhart, Indiana, has edited
*Freedom and Discipleship: Liberation Theology in an
Anabaptist Perspective,*[1] a volume of essays by Latin
American and North American theologians from the
Anabaptist-Mennonite tradition that includes responses
by Protestant liberation theologians.

In the pages that follow, I want to explore the possibility of such a dialogue for us in North America. Rather
than concentrating on one particular confession, I have
chosen to focus more broadly on central elements in the
reinterpretation of the gospel by the Lutheran, Calvinist,
and Anabaptist Reformers. In such a preliminary exploration, I can only hope to suggest an approach and a process

that can be carried much further by others, especially by small faith communities engaged in such an effort at re-creation.

I began this project five years ago when I was invited to conduct a seminar called "Protestantism and Liberation" in the Theological Workshop sponsored by the Departamento Ecuménico de Investigaciónes for priests, pastors, women religious, and lay leaders from various countries in Central and South America and the Caribbean who are involved in the "popular church." My participation in this Workshop each year since then provided me with an excellent opportunity to discuss my thought and writing as they developed. In February 1990, I gave the George Casalis Lectures on this same topic at the Centro Intereclesial de Estudios Teológicos y Sociales, a Protestant seminary in Managua, Nicaragua.

The response of those who participated in these discussions has contributed a great deal to the clarification and development of my thought; it has also convinced me that this engagement with the Reformation of the sixteenth century can be of value for both Catholics and Protestants. Such an encounter can help those of us who are Protestants get a better sense of who we are and can equip us to live our faith more dynamically. And Roman Catholics may discover that a liberation movement so deeply rooted in the Catholic tradition has something to offer another dynamic movement rooted in that same heritage today.

The initiative for reformations in the past has come not primarily from executives, scholars, and pastors at the center of the church's life but from those on the margin, not from those involved in the preservation of a religious institution but from those who are closer to the suffering and struggle of their time, who strive to relate their faith to that suffering and respond to that struggle with their lives. I believe that this is amply demonstrated today as well, as those living in solidarity with the poor and oppressed and involved in some way in the struggle for justice and peace seek to deepen their faith and live in community. Here I address primarily such persons: lay women and men, pastors and seminarians, priests and women religious. With them in mind, I have attempted to deal with fundamental theological issues while avoiding, as much as possible, the use of abstract theological categories and reasoning.

R.S.

Introduction

Christian churches, like other historical movements, become institutionalized. When this happens, those in positions of leadership in those churches spend most of their energies working for their efficient functioning and their self-preservation. Eventually, this repetition of past responses to a changing human situation can lead to stagnation, sclerosis, and death. But even that threat may not be enough to bring about renewal. This was brought home to me forcefully some years ago when I dared to call the attention of a distinguished official of a major Protestant denomination to what I considered such a danger. I shall never forget his reply: "I know that my church is dying. But as long as I am in the position I hold in it, my responsibility is to keep it functioning as efficiently as possible."

Christianity has also demonstrated, time and time again, an extraordinary capacity to renew and re-create itself, as it responds to new challenges and gives birth to new movements. This possibility of going against and overcoming the logic of institutions and thus opening the way to ongoing transformation is a logical consequence of the faith by which the church lives: faith in a God who transcends yet is active in history in order to transform the kingdoms of this world into the reign of God; faith in Jesus Christ, who challenged this process of sclerosis and death by living out an alternative, a pattern of death (the giving up of everything, including his life) leading to resurrection (the new and unexpected life emerging out of death), thus becoming the head of a community of women and men who are set free from bondage to the past in order to die and rise again with him daily; faith in the Holy Spirit, present in the church as the Spirit of innovation, calling and leading the church into new pathways of obedience in response to new human challenges.

Thus, on many occasions when the institutional church has been unfaithful to this faith heritage, some of those who have been nourished by it turn to the Bible, are grasped by this divine reality, and discover the gospel as a new message speaking directly to their situation. In response to this message, they find new life, live an experience that reorients them in the world, and form a new community as this subversive memory takes hold of them and shapes them. Thus they become instruments of a Power that calls forth new incarnations of the Spirit, breaks the hold of the stagnation that comes with repetition, and creates new forms of life. They participate in a community of faith whose radically different approach to history and society makes them capable of transforming their world. They enable us to see that we are most faithful to our past as it has been expressed in institutions and structures when we struggle to transform them, drawing on a Power that calls us into a new future.

We can look at the church from this perspective of its reinvention because it is happening today. Liberation theology and the Christian base communities in Latin America are one expression of it. In these small communities, poor and marginal women and men gather to read and study the Bible. As they do so, they are captivated by a clear and compelling message: God is acting redemptively in history to liberate the oppressed and to establish the reign of God, in which those at the bottom will be the privileged ones. They experience powerfully the presence of Jesus Christ in the midst of this struggle, giving them life and hope. Living this newfound faith, they create a new model of the church, an *ecclesiola in ecclesia* ("little church within the church"), as such communities have often been called. Sustained by their faith and their life together, they are becoming a significant force for the transformation of their society.

From this vantage point, we can also see more clearly how often such movements of the Spirit have emerged in Christian history and how much we owe to them. In these pages, we will focus on one of them, the Reformation of the sixteenth century, which has profoundly affected all of us, Catholic as well as Protestant, and played a major role in shaping our modern world. Like liberation theology and the Christian base communities, this movement emerged at a time of crisis in the church and in society. Martin Luther, Ulrich Zwingli, John Calvin, and the Anabaptist reformers were all persons who experienced this crisis in the depth of their being and, in their anguish, turned to the Bible. Reading it in the midst of their struggle, they were grasped by a message they had never heard before— the incredible good news of God's gracious gift of forgiveness and justification. As they received this gift, they had a new and rich experience of the presence of Christ, giving them life. As their eyes were opened, they discovered new dimensions of the biblical story and found themselves engaged in a reinterpretation of their entire heritage of faith. And a new experience of faith brought into being a new community, which lived out a new quality of life in the world.

You and I may belong to religious institutions that have settled into a process of repetition and stagnation. But our faith connects us with a Power capable of breaking this bondage and bringing life out of death. We also have before us the experience and witness of those who have found the vision and strength they needed to undertake this work of re-formation in the past as well as today. In dialogue with them we may catch a new vision of what it might mean for us to do something similar in our situation. We may also find that they, through their experience and reflection, have much to offer us. Elements of our religious heritage, taken for granted for centuries and imprisoned in static doctrinal statements, may take on new meaning as we explore them and reinterpret them in our struggle to reform the church. Other elements, ignored or lost, may be rediscovered.

In the chapters that follow, I will look at four central themes of the Protestant Reformation and will attempt to grasp more clearly what they contributed to the struggle for liberation and the reinvention of the church in the sixteenth century. In examining each theme, I also want to explore what that particular understanding and experience of the gospel can offer us today, if we are engaged in a similar struggle where we find ourselves. These themes are: (1) Martin Luther's spiritual pilgrimage and his discovery of God's gracious gift of forgiveness and justification by faith; (2) the Bible open to all, a liberating and life-giving Word directly accessible to the people; (3) the vision of a reformed church always undergoing reformation, an *ecclesia reformata semper reformanda*, along with the Protestant principle, which undercut all attempts to sacralize the established order and thus directed the Christian life toward the radical transformation of society; and (4) the rejection of the church-state relations of Christendom by the Anabaptists and their call to radical discipleship.

I have chosen these four elements because I believe that they represent four major contributions of the Reformation in the sixteenth century that are important for us today. I realize that they represent only a small part of the richness of that movement of the Spirit and that I have hardly scratched the surface in my exploration of it. But I dare to present here the results of my attempt at a dialogue with the Reformation from the perspective of liberation theology in order to propose an approach and a project which I believe should be taken up not only by scholars but also by communities of faith, especially those closely identified with the struggle of marginal and oppressed people.

I realize that no single movement in the Reformation

gave a central place to these four major themes. In developing them, I have drawn on traditions that not only went their separate ways but also found themselves, at times, in conflict with each other. But, over the centuries, these major contributions of the Reformation have become part of our heritage. They have shaped us and are available to all of us as a resource on which we can draw as we seek to find our way.

As I engage in this dialogue with the Protestant Reformation from the perspective of the New Reformation taking place today, I am more convinced than ever of the importance of learning what history can teach us and of struggling with the question of how best to appropriate those lessons. I am also very much aware of my own limitations: I have not been trained as a historian. And while, over the years, I have turned time and again to the writings of Martin Luther, John Calvin, and the Radical Reformers, other academic pursuits have had higher priority. At the same time, as a missionary and theologian, I have always sought to draw on the theological heritage flowing from the Reformation in order to live and act in the present. And I have learned that I can best explore and draw on that heritage as I direct new questions to it, questions shaped at least in part by the challenges I am facing. I have also found that my appropriation of the lessons of history has a dialogical dimension to it; I draw on it as I carry on a dialogue within myself between the heritage of faith, which is both a part of me and something I continue to appropriate, and the dynamic situation in which I am involved.

Because I approach the Reformation from this perspective, I have no desire to claim that it was a movement for political liberation like those occurring in our time. Nor am I particularly interested in finding precedents in it for social and political actions that might be important today. I see the Reformation as fundamentally a movement of *spiritual* liberation, which cut to the heart of the struggle for liberation from oppression in that time and place and which, by its very nature, had wide implications for many

other areas of life. For Luther, this experience of liberation through justification by faith was so tremendous that
he gave little attention to the task of working out its
implications for the social and political realms. A similar
experience of this profound spiritual reality led Calvin to
strive for the total transformation and ordering of society
under the Word of God. But what he did along these lines
was directly related to the new world emerging at the end
of the feudal era and to the aspirations of the new social
class of that time, the bourgeoisie, not to the emergence of
the poor as the new historical subject, as is happening
today.

At the same time, the more I explore that movement of
spiritual liberation, the more convinced I am of the
contribution it has made across the centuries, both to the
ongoing reformation of the church and to the continuing
struggle for social transformation. And precisely when I
accept it for what it was, as I am involved in struggles for
reformation and liberation today, I find that it serves to
orient me and to provide resources for critical participation in such reformative movements in both church and
society. The pages that follow represent my attempt to
carry on this sort of dialogue and learn from it.

There is one other dimension of the Reformation of the
sixteenth century that is also present in today's New
Reformation: the conviction, on the part of the Reformers,
that the gospel message by which they had been grasped
represented a new and compelling message that called for
new responses in all areas of the church's life and witness.
It provided them with what we might call today a new
paradigm or hermeneutical principle through which they
engaged in a rereading not only of the Bible but of the
entire theological tradition. Justification by faith represented, for Luther, the heart of the gospel, a message he
found on almost every page of the Bible, and he proceeded
to reinterpret not only the Bible but the great theologians
of the past in the light of it. For liberation theologians,
God's concern for the poor and marginal and God's dynamic action in history to offer liberation in the fullest

sense provide a similar paradigm for a rereading of the Bible and the theological tradition.

Whenever such a new paradigm emerges and takes hold, it creates a new situation in the church that calls for a realignment of forces. Old differences and divisions become secondary, even those created by an earlier reformation. At the same time, Christians formerly separated are surprised by a new experience of unity and solidarity. As a result of Luther's rediscovery of justification by faith and his vigorous defense of it, laypersons as well as priests and scholars found themselves forced to respond positively or negatively; new and often surprising alignments were formed on both sides.

Today, by the same token, the new paradigm of liberation theology lays before us the clear gospel message of liberation in such a way that a decision for or against it is required. The result is a new alignment that transcends former confessional divisions, including the one between Catholics and Protestants.

New alignments are also beginning to happen in many places in Latin America, to the surprise of many. There, traditionally, Catholics and Protestants have had practically no contact with each other. Each Protestant denomination has tended to go its own way, and in recent years the lines have been sharply drawn between mainline Protestant and Pentecostal churches. But as Christians in these various confessions are disturbed by the suffering and death around them, hear the gospel message of liberation, and experience the transforming presence of the Holy Spirit in the base communities, they find themselves united, in their faith and in their struggle, with others who have undergone a similar experience of conversion. Thus Catholics and Protestants living on this frontier of mission find that they are closer to each other than they are to members of their own confession who have not responded to this call. Likewise, members of the mainline Protestant churches and Pentecostals who respond to the moving of the Spirit have a similar experience of a new ecumenical reality.

Challenged by the theology of liberation to look for signs of the inbreaking of the reign of God in our midst and to respond to the leading of the Spirit in our time and place, we can perceive the limitations of our past and the tremendous task of re-creation ahead of us. As we strive to articulate the meaning of the gospel for this situation and to create a new model of church, we realize how much we can learn from each other. As we work together at this task, we also help each other discover more of the riches in our own particular heritage. And as we face mounting opposition, if not persecution, in the church as well as in society, we know that we can be faithful to our calling only as we learn how to support each other.

I'm convinced that this new ecumenical experience among those who seek to re-form the church from the perspective of the theology of liberation and liberation struggles today is especially important for North American Protestants, for we have been an integral part of Western bourgeois culture and society and feel at home in it. Our churches have occupied a privileged position in that society and, by and large, help to legitimate society. Our theology has been largely worked out in the academy by white men decisively influenced by Greek and German ways of thinking who are very much a part of the established order.

Consequently, this heritage of faith can speak to the urgent human issues and struggles of our time only as we are able to look at it more critically, free it from its present bondage to oppressive structures, and discover how to express it in a new language, new commitments, and a new community. The initiative for this may well come from those who, until now, have been kept at the margins of our churches: women, those of other races and cultures, and those who have been oppressed by the established order of which the church is an integral part. Only as Protestantism undergoes a process of death and resurrection, which must find expression in new communities of faith that transcend traditional confessional lines, will it contribute to the transformation of the world of the future as it has the past. I'm convinced that Protestantism has this potential and that a new engagement with the Reformation of the sixteenth century, in the light of the challenge of a New Reformation, can contribute significantly to the church's renewal.

1

Luther and Liberation

Luther brought about a grand process of liberation. He will always be a necessary point of reference for all who seek liberation and know how to struggle and suffer for it.

Leonardo Boff[1]

The sixteenth century in western Europe represented the propitious moment and the right place for the emergence of a liberation movement grounded in the Christian faith. It was a time of rapid social change, as the feudal system was eroding under the impact of new economic, social, and cultural forces. In 1500, nine out of every ten people in Europe were living on the land and were sustained by it. Peasants had been smarting under oppression for centuries, and their rebellions became more frequent as the feudal system lost some of its power. Moreover, new cities were emerging in which a new social class, made up of artisans, bankers, businessmen, lawyers, and teachers, was coming to the fore. They, along with others, constituted a new "middle" class, people who were not bound to the land and whose horizons were not determined by the limits of the feudal world.

In fact, their horizons were expanding at a fantastic speed. Explorers traveling to Africa, the Orient, and America called attention to the existence of vast spaces inhabited by peoples of cultures and races hitherto largely unknown. Greater movement of people by land and by sea created new opportunities for trade and commerce. The invention of the printing press by Johannes Gutenberg made past thought accessible to persons outside of monasteries and other narrow circles and greatly facilitated the rapid communication of ideas and events. And the recovery of the literature and philosophy of antiquity, especially of the Greeks, put people in touch with exciting new dimensions of human life and thought.

In the midst of all this ferment, many men and women were dominated by tremendous fear, anxiety, and insecurity. The new world opening before them was completely unknown, a world with which they were not prepared to cope. The ground under their feet, which had seemed so solid for centuries, was giving way; everything in which they once trusted for safety was being called into question. At the same time the bourgeoisie, the new class emerging primarily in the cities, felt confined and oppressed by the structures and the worldview of the feudal society and were excited by the new ideas swirling around them. They were developing a new vision of society. No longer bound to the past, they could dream of a new future and struggle for it.

The Role of the Church in an Oppressive Society

At that point in history, the struggle for liberation had to be essentially a religious struggle. Within the framework of medieval Christendom, the church was at the center of society, and religion provided the milieu in which women and men lived and moved and had their being. God and the struggle for salvation, within the sacramental system of the church, constituted the symbolic world around which people ordered their earthly pilgrimage. And this religion, both in its spirit and its institutional expressions, rather than being a force of liberation, was the keystone of the arch that sustained the whole system of domination and oppression. Three aspects of it stand out.

1. The church was an integral part of the dominant economic and political systems and used its economic and political power as well as its spiritual influence to support those systems. In a fascinating article, "Luther Between the Reformation and Liberation," the well-known Brazilian Catholic priest Leonardo Boff describes the medieval European church:

> In semifeudal and mercantilist Europe of the fifteenth and sixteenth centuries, the church was a fundamental part of the structure. The Roman See and the bishops, especially in Germany, had great economic, political, juridical and military interests. It should not be forgotten that the Pope had great temporal power with innumerable treaties and benefits. In the semifeudal and mercantile bourgeois order, there existed relations of vassals and subjects, lords and servants, colonizers and colonized. More concretely, religious persuasion as well as armed coercion were used to keep the peasants in submission, despite frequent uprisings in Bohemia, Swabia, France and other parts of central Europe. The feudal aristocracy and the mercantilist bourgeois society worked out a pact with the clergy (who also had secular power) so that the church became the central factor in the reproduction of the semifeudal and mercantilist society. Thus the church, in its multifunctional nature, consecrated and solidified the relations of the *status quo,* which were relations of domination.[2]

2. Much of the theology of the medieval church contributed to the sacralization of this social order and thus served to give divine legitimation to it. God, conceived of with the aid of philosophical categories taken from the Greeks, was understood as the Supreme Being, and this divine reality descended into the cosmos and society through hierarchical structures. Theologians influenced by neo-Platonic thought, with its conception of a chain of being, assumed that the hierarchical structure of society possessed a sacred character; it belonged to an eternal order of being that could not be questioned or changed.

While this notion did not go unchallenged in medieval thought, it was widely accepted by theologians as well as by the faithful. In this context, faith in God meant accepting the established order as divine as well as submitting to that order.

The structure of the church was conceived of in a similar way, except that the church possessed even more of this divine reality. Here, too, something like a ladder of being existed, a hierarchy that flowed downward from God through Christ to the pope, bishops, and priests. In a sense, they constituted the church, leaving the mass of ordinary believers completely at the margins. And this institution, hierarchically structured, was permeated with the divine. Existing side by side with the civil structures, in charge of its own often vast economic and political realm, the church provided a theological rationale that sustained the feudal society; the church's structure, as well as the spirit that it fostered, provided the symbolic system within which feudal society was taken for granted.

3. The real power of domination, which sustained this entire system, was manifested in the spiritual realm by the domination of the spirit of the people through the hierarchical-sacramental system. The truth about God, conceived of as the Absolute, was revealed in true doctrine, given objectively and suprapersonally through the hierarchy, and meant to be received and accepted uncritically by believers. And the grace of God, offering salvation and sustaining the believer throughout his life, was made available to all through the sacraments.

It may be difficult for us today, whether we are Catholic or Protestant, to fully understand the hold that this system had over the people. The medieval world was a profoundly religious world. All of life was centered on God and the striving for eternal salvation. And much had been done by spiritual leaders over the centuries to portray not only the urgency of this quest but the possibility of getting lost along the way. God was seen as the judge who demanded righteousness; the devil was strong, and many were the temptations to fall into mortal sin and depart from the path of salvation. But the church was present in the midst of all this, offering a sure way, a secure path, by means of the seven sacraments, which mediated God's grace at all the crucial moments in the journey from birth to death. And the church, through the priesthood, had complete control over these sacraments and thus over the people. Grace flowed into the life of the believer through the sacraments, when properly administered by a priest. Herein lay the priests'—and the hierarchy's—power over the people. And as long as people were supremely concerned about their eternal salvation and were convinced that grace was available to them only through this means, they were oppressed in the core of their beings and there could be no liberation until that domination was broken.

This is why Martin Luther emerged as the great liberator in sixteenth-century Europe. As a profoundly religious person, whose absorbing passion was finding a right relation to God and being assured of salvation, Luther became acutely aware of something that others around him were beginning to realize. There was a fatal flaw in the system: It did not provide the certainty of salvation it promised. And in the midst of his anguish, as he studied the scriptures, Luther discovered another route, a route that offered a viable alternative to the sacerdotal-sacramental system. Because of this discovery, he brought about what Leonard Boff has called "a grand process of liberation."[3]

The Struggle and Liberating Discovery of Luther

Luther, born in 1483, early on found himself obsessed with the problem of living at peace with God. In his struggle to find a solution, he entered an Augustinian monastery, where he soon stood out because of the intensity of his spiritual discipline and the fervor of his striving for a security that escaped his grasp. In his desperation, he turned to the Bible. But his reading of it only heightened his anxiety as he found himself confronted by a sovereign God present and active everywhere, a God of justice who demanded complete obedience. Luther found himself completely incapable of such obedience; in fact, the stronger his sense of the reality of this God of justice, the more aware he was of his complete inability to follow this path of obedience. As a result, he soon concluded that God was terribly angry with him. His intensified spiritual sensitivity led him to believe himself a person accused and accursed, with no consolation, a person condemned to eternal damnation from which he could find no possible escape.

In his anguish, he followed the route through the sacraments prescribed by the church, to no avail. No matter how hard he tried, he could not attain his goal. The grace mediated through the sacraments did not change his desperate situation. Time and time again, he went to confession, seeking absolution of his sins. But no act of penance could compensate for the fact that, moments later, he might commit a mortal sin and thus once again be in danger of losing his salvation.

In the midst of this overwhelming anguish, as Luther immersed himself in the Psalms and the epistles of Paul, something extraordinary broke through to him and took him completely by surprise: This God, who demands justice, is a God who forgives. In fact, the *justice* of God is manifested precisely in forgiveness. The just God is the God who loves, who shows mercy, who comes to us in Christ in order to forgive, accept, and save us. And this love and mercy are so great that God is willing to give God's son for us. As Paul put it, "while we were yet sinners Christ died for us" (Rom. 5:8). In the presence of God, Christ stands in our place.

According to Leonardo Boff, Luther thus "celebrated the incredible discovery of the unlimited mercy of God in Jesus Christ crucified,"[4] The impossible problem of trying to justify oneself before God, to which Luther could find no solution, has been solved—*by God*. God takes the initiative in coming to us. God approaches us directly, without intermediaries. And God offers us, freely, everything of which we are incapable; we are not only forgiven but stand before God justified. And all this is daily available to us, on one condition alone: that we dare to accept it, trusting completely in the promises of this God. In other words, that we live by faith.

For Luther, and others who responded to this message, this meant an extraordinary experience of liberation: liberation from the fear of God and from all anxiety about salvation; liberation in the very core of their beings, as they were able to look honestly at their own weaknesses and shortcomings, errors and sins, and know that the hold of all these things over them had been broken by God's gift of forgiveness; liberation from the burden of enslavement to rules and obligations, as God empowered them to love as Jesus Christ had loved; and liberation from domination by priests or political rulers, who claimed power over them in God's name.

In other words, Luther and the other Reformers took what was at the heart of the spiritual preoccupation of the time and reaffirmed it by radically reinterpreting it: God-consciousness, the sense of God's presence everywhere, which had become a source of fear, anxiety, and oppression, suddenly became a source of life and hope. The spiritual journey was, once again, an exciting adventure. And this powerful spiritual awakening brought religious faith once again into the center of life and led to the revitalization of culture as well.

For the Reformers, God was indeed at the very center of human existence, active everywhere in history, constantly taking the initiative in approaching human beings. But at the heart of God's activity is the forgiveness of sins and the gracious offer of new life to those who dare to trust and respond. Thus life can be lived fully and dynamically in this milieu as a daily response, in gratitude for this gift. As John Calvin put it in a letter to King Francis I of France, "What is more consonant with faith than to recognize that we are naked of all virtue, in order to be clothed by God? That we are empty of all good, to be filled by him? That we are slaves of sin, to be freed by him?

Blind, to be illumined by him? Lame, to be made straight by him? Weak, to be sustained by him?"[5]

Luther's discovery marked the opening of a new era in the human struggle for liberation by freeing women and men from bondage at the center of their beings, transforming the church into a liberated zone—a space in which this liberation could be lived out—and empowering those thus liberated for dynamic action in society. Several dimensions of this new reality stand out in bold relief.

God's Gracious Initiative: Source of New Life

Men and women who had been immobilized by fear, locked into a closed world, and oppressed by external powers in church and in society were freed from these burdens as they encountered a new source of life. They thus found themselves living in a new space that encouraged the development of their personalities and gave direction to their new energies, a space that provided them with a new opportunity to became "subjects" of their own lives and struggles, to use a term now common in third-world liberation struggles.

I had a new sense of what this must have meant for many at that time as I recently took part in an intensive workshop that focused on personal growth and the cultivation of interpersonal relationships. Those who took part in it were helped to identify clearly things out of their pasts and in their personalities that kept them from living fully. They also began to get more in touch with resources and energies within themselves that they could draw on to overcome these obstacles. And as they helped each other draw on these resources, a new world of possibilities for their personal and professional lives opened before them, and they felt themselves propelled forward by energies they did not know they had.

Something similar to this must have happened to the men and women in sixteenth-century Europe as their understanding of and relationship with God were dramatically transformed and became a source of new life.

1. This God forgives us and sets us right. Christ is not only for us but in us, supporting us and giving us life every day, in spite of our limits and failures. Paul goes so far as to say that, in the new life he lives, "it is no longer I who live, but Christ who lives in me" (Gal. 2:20). Each person is free to center her life on the acceptance of this gift and on the exploration of the limitless possibilities it offers. God is like the sun, which we cannot control but which is always there to give us light and warmth. What we can do is condition our bodies and our lives so as to take the fullest advantage of all that is offered us. Thus, on our spiritual journey, we are set free from undue introspection. Like other religious persons, we are concerned about our spiritual state, about those times when faith may be at a low ebb, and about our failure to love or to practice justice. But we struggle with these issues in the context of God's amazing gift of grace, which frees us to concentrate all our energies on serving God and neighbor and gives us the courage and strength to continue striving.

2. God approaches us directly, not through intermediaries. And because this God is gracious, we can dare to stand before God in a relationship of immediacy. Only the Word and the sacraments stand between us and God, but they serve to make real this direct relationship, not to distance us from God. Thus, a personal relationship with God in Christ becomes the central reality of Protestant spirituality.

3. In this context, the believer is set free from bondage to self to focus on the reign of God. Overwhelmed by God's gift, he can only express gratitude for this gift of love by loving others. As Luther wrote in *A Treatise on Christian Liberty,* "As our heavenly Father has in Christ freely come to our help, we also ought freely to help our neighbor through our body and its works, and each should become as it were a Christ to the other."[6] "A Christian man lives not in himself, but in Christ and in his neighbor. He lives in Christ through faith, in his neighbor through love."[7] Consequently, the Christian life is a life of extraordinary freedom, freedom that finds its most authentic expression

in the decision to give life for others. In Luther's words, "A Christian man is a perfectly free lord of all, subject to none. A Christian man is a perfectly dutiful servant of all, subject to all."[8]

A New Source of Authority

Through his discovery and experience of justification by faith, Luther completely undermined the system that gave the church, its hierarchy, and its priests control over the people, thus opening the way for the emergence of those at the bottom as responsible Subjects.

A merciful God offers the forgiveness and grace necessary to transform life to everyone who hears the Word and believes in the promise presented in Word and sacrament. All this is offered directly. There is no need for any person or institution to mediate this grace; in fact, any attempt at mediation would only interfere with a full reception of and response to grace. Moreover, authority does not reside in a visible institution but in the Word of God, interpreted by conscience. All believers, whatever their position in church or society, are approached directly by the God who offers them forgiveness and life. They are addressed in their consciences and thus can make a personal decision that no one else dares make for them. They are capable of trusting their own experience of faith, of reading the Bible and understanding it, and of finding the path of obedience. As Luther wrote in *The Babylonian Captivity of the Church,* "Where there is a divine promise every one must stand upon his own feet, every one's personal faith is demanded, every one will give an account for himself and will bear his own burden."[9]

Inevitably, this breakthrough exposed the paternalism of the medieval religious system and offered an alternative to it. Much has been written over the centuries, by Catholics as well as by Protestants, about the way in which medieval Catholicism tended to take care of the faithful, to protect them from too many disturbances of conscience, from too much anxiety, and from the burden of too much responsibility. The sacerdotal-sacramental system took care of their relationship with God by defining the correct doctrine for them, spelling out clearly their religious duties, and prescribing how they should live in society.

In contrast, as did Luther, those who receive God's gracious gift know no such sheltered space or comfortable spiritual situation, nor do they want it. Responding directly to God's initiative, they are like children who have grown up and thus no longer need to be dependent on a father and mother. They are called on every day to be responsible human beings, as they struggle with the uncertainties of faith, receive forgiveness, demonstrate gratitude in service to others, and struggle against all the forces of evil around them. This makes for a strenuous life, lived in the midst of uncertainties, from which many Protestants tend to flee. (This is the appeal of fundamentalism, especially in times of crisis.) But it is also a way of life in which each person, whatever her position in the world, is encouraged to stand tall, live fully, and act responsibly.

Standing on this solid spiritual foundation, Luther was able to take another step that has contributed mightily to the struggle for liberation in the modern world. As a humble and unknown monk, holding no position of authority in the church, he dared to stand up to those in the highest positions in church and society who claimed that their authority had come from God.

Luther's experience of forgiveness and justification was so profound and so compelling that he could not doubt that it was at the heart of the gospel. Turning to the Bible, which the church considered to be the ultimate source of divine revelation, he found that message on almost every page. His experience and his reading of the Bible confirmed his conviction that God approached believers directly through their consciences. Thus when princes and the emperor as well as bishops and the pope began to denounce and persecute him, demanding that he retract, he responded, "I cannot and will not retract, for it is neither good nor sincere to go against one's conscience. May God help me. Amen."

If we take into account the attitude toward secular and religious authority dominant in sixteenth-century Europe, it is hard to exaggerate the radicalism of this step. As was pointed out earlier, it was taken for granted that the established order in society was part of an eternal order of being given by God and that those in power were there by divine right. In the church, the pope and bishops were considered Christ's representatives, whose authority could not be questioned. And those who aspired to the priesthood were subjected to many years of spiritual and intellectual training and discipline to fit into this system. And yet Luther, totally integrated into that world, was convinced that the truth of the gospel by which he had been grasped and the voice of God speaking to him through his conscience were so compelling that no human authority in society or in the church could make him doubt it or could control him.

By this stance, Luther set in motion forces that have profoundly affected the struggles for liberation on the part of oppressed people to this day. He made it possible for Christians to question and undermine the claims of secular rulers that their authority was somehow sacred and must be respected uncritically. By challenging assumptions about the nature of authority in the church, Luther provided an impetus for movements of radical renewal and thus helped create space for the emergence of new patterns of community and new models of church. And he encouraged the development of communities of faith capable of confronting and resisting demonic powers and, in some situations, of supporting revolutionary struggles.

Several decades later, Calvin provided theological undergirding for this stance with his emphases on the sovereignty of God and the calling of Christians to always render obedience to God over any secular authority. This stance led to Puritan participation in the English Revolution (1642–1648) and has sustained resistance movements

in Nazi Germany, in present-day South Africa, and elsewhere.

The Priesthood of All Believers

By proclaiming the universal priesthood of all believers, Luther not only made it impossible for one group in
the church to keep others in an inferior position but also
raised up all believers, including those considered most
lowly, to the privileged position of the priest.

There can be no higher position in the church than that
of the believer who receives Christ's tremendous gift of
forgiveness and justification. Anyone who accepts it
gratefully is chosen by God and raised up to a unique
position. Moreover, there can be no higher calling than
that given to every believer to transmit this message,
with its offer of life to others, and to express this faith in
loving service to others. And this message is so simple and
clear that anyone can understand and announce it because it is presented to us in the Bible, in the language of
the people. And this truth, as understood by simple
people, is a more faithful expression of the gospel than
were the fine distinctions of the classical debates of
theologians or the abstract language of the christological
formulations of the fourth century.

As a bearer of this message of forgiveness, every
Christian becomes a priest. In the words of Luther, the
Christian is "a Christ to the other," able to stand before
God, to announce the word of forgiveness, to pray for
others, and to teach them the things of God. Each believer
is "able to do all things which we see done and prefigured
in the outward and visible works of priests."[10]

Luther went even further. He claimed that God has
called every Christian to serve his neighbor, to actualize
love in the world. This is the fundamental, the highest
possible vocation of the Christian. Consequently, the life
of the humblest believer living and working in the secular
world is as important before God as that of any priest; the
mystique formerly attached to the ascetic life of the

religious (that is, a member of a religious order) is here transferred to all Christians. And this calling, for Luther, applied to all, including those at the bottom of the social ladder: "The world does not know the hidden treasures of God. It cannot be persuaded that the maid working obediently and the servant faithfully performing his duty, or the woman rearing her children, are as good as the praying monk who beats his breast and wrestles with his spirit."[11]

Every believer is a priest, capable of making the gospel and its benefits available to others. But, for the sake of the effective functioning of the church, some persons have to be chosen and commissioned to do this for the whole body, to assume this special stewardship for the body. Thus a specific ministry was called for that included preaching and teaching, administering the sacraments, pronouncing the message of forgiveness, and taking on certain pastoral functions. Such ministries came to be seen as callings to proclaim a life-giving and world-transforming message, to serve rather than have power over others. As a result, a new and compelling vision of ministry emerged, capable of appealing to those most profoundly affected by this message. And as the emerging new church had no political power and no privileged economic position, these new ministers had no special status in society and often had to live in poverty with their families, resorting to farming and, at times, to begging in order to survive. Such a calling held little appeal to people from the privileged classes but instead opened the way for those formerly excluded from the priesthood to take positions of leadership in the church.

Spiritual Liberation and Social Transformation

Luther's struggle for liberation was, as we have seen, a religious struggle, carried on within the bounds of the church. But those men and women who underwent this profound spiritual transformation began to look at the world around them in a new way and to act differently. In so doing, they not only contributed decisively to the shaping of our modern world but also helped to lay the foundation for our liberation struggles today.

1. By his emphases on God's direct relationship with each individual person and on the centrality of each person's response of faithful service to her neighbor, Luther opened the way for those at the bottom of the social ladder to have a new sense of self-worth and to emerge as responsible individuals.

2. His emphasis upon the believer's right and obligation to listen to the Word and to obey the voice of conscience led to the emancipation of human reason from bondage to religious authorities and dogmas. This created a new space for women and men to think for themselves as well as to demand freedom of speech and the right to make decisions about their lives and destinies, individually and collectively.

3. In Germany, the Lutheran Reformation laid the foundation for a new integration of society and for the formation of the state. Before Luther, Germany was divided into civil and religious units, some governed by canonical law, others by civil law. The church owned and ruled over vast land holdings, and the clergy often disputed political offices with civil authorities. In this situation, Luther succeeded in uniting the people around the office of the high magistrate, under whose rule the nation was organized and society was integrated as never before. Moreover, with his emphasis upon the calling of those in public office, Luther gave an important place in society to and provided religious motivation for a new social class: "The drab, grey life of the average bureaucrat was suddenly transformed, as if by a great volcanic eruption. . . . The civil servant became a proud, leading character, the torch-bearer of a special form of European life, an organized unit."[12]

4. A religious experience of liberation, lived in a new community of faith, had a tremendous appeal to a new social class; at the same time, this experience of faith turned attention toward the future and made it possible

for Protestants to respond positively to the new spirit stirring in culture and society. Thus many Protestants were able to play a creative role in the struggles shaping the modern Western world in the realms of intellectual freedom and scientific achievement, in the development of democratic institutions within the nation-state, and in commercial and industrial growth.

2

The Lutheran Reformation and Liberation Today

In the preceding chapter, we outlined the contribution Martin Luther made to the liberation struggle in the sixteenth century. That heritage has made its impact far beyond Germany and the time in which Luther lived, so much so that it has become a part of our common history. At the same time, the Lutheran Reformation, as a force for liberation in history, was seriously limited from the beginning by a number of factors.

1. Luther himself was not able to see clearly or work out conceptually the implications of his spiritual revolution for the social and political realms. Nor was he able to define precisely the role of the church in the new situation he had helped to create.

2. Caught in a situation in which the Reformation, in order to survive, had to depend upon the support of the princes and other political leaders, Luther allowed those in power in the state to have an important role in the life of the church and opened the way for the Lutheran Church, a product of this Reformation, to become another state church.

3. When the oppressed peasants, partly encouraged by what Luther had done, rose up in revolt, Luther at first supported them against their rulers. But when he concluded that the Peasants' War (1524–1526) was getting out of control and was threatening the Reformation, he

41

not only denounced the peasants but urged those in power to suppress them. As a result, the Lutheran Church in Germany lost its opportunity to stand in solidarity with the poor, became the church of the emerging bourgeoisie and lived, more or less, at ease with those in power. To be sure, by taking this stance the Lutheran Church allied itself with what was, at the time, a progressive if not revolutionary force. But the church largely ignored its calling to take a critical stance against that order and thus lost its ability to relate creatively later to new movements for liberation.

4. This Reformation failed to create, within itself, conditions for its own reformation. Unable to re-create the founding experience in new generations, the Lutheran Church failed to respond to the innovative work of the Holy Spirit in new historical situations. Thus, early on, it fell into the same type of institutional rigidity against which Luther had been compelled to rebel. This church of the Reformation also became all too concerned about its own self-preservation and, therefore, allowed the old sacralization of authority it had denounced in Catholicism to creep back in and take over. Consequently, the church lost touch with new forces of transformation in society and failed to connect with new social classes emerging in later centuries; movements of spiritual renewal were marginalized or forced to go their own independent ways.

The Christian Base Communities
and the Reactivation of This Heritage

The Lutheran Reformation was a tremendous force for liberation in sixteenth-century Europe. But can it contribute to a New Reformation today, transforming the church into a force for liberation in our world? I'm convinced that it can. For those of us who are Protestants, the Reformation is an integral part of our social autobiography that helps make us who we are. It can serve to orient and to empower us today, on one condition: that it be reactivated. And it will be reactivated, as we dare to situate ourselves on the frontier of the human struggle of our time, as Luther did in his, and allow ourselves to be grasped by the good news of the gospel as it breaks through to us now. In response to the present call for reformation, this heritage of the first Reformation will come alive again for us.

At this point we have one great advantage over Luther. We don't have to go through an agonizing struggle for years, as he did, to find that message and reality for our time. We now know that the frontier of God's redemptive action is where the vast numbers of poor and oppressed peoples of the world are. We have already discovered that the God we worship is working dynamically in their midst, offering them life. For this God is the God who liberated slaves from Egypt, the God proclaimed by the Hebrew prophets as the God of justice for the poor, the God of Jesus of Nazareth, whose life and witness centered on the reign of God, a new order of life breaking in, in which the poor would be the privileged. We see manifestations of the presence and power of God among the poor, as they live a new quality of life together in the Christian base communities. Remaining within and loyal to the institutional church, these communities provide a new model of church capable of challenging and renewing it.

This knowledge, now available to us as our starting point, is a new paradigm, capable of empowering us to do in our time what Luther did in his, using a newly grasped biblical Word that equips us to re-create the compelling spiritual experience in which Protestantism was born and thus rediscover the power of our Reformation heritage in the struggle for liberation today. Along with it, we have the witness of the Christian base communities to the work of the Holy Spirit, bringing into existence "a little church within the church" not only among the poor but also among those who stand with them in their struggle for justice. As we respond to this Word in community, I believe that several elements at the heart of the Lutheran Reformation will come alive for us in a new way.

1. We will have a new experience of a direct relationship with a loving and merciful God as we meet this God in

history, where this God is and has always been present—among poor and marginal people, in the heart of the struggle for life over against structures of domination and oppression, and in the midst of suffering and persecution for the cause of justice. Since many of us who frequent mainline churches are far removed from these places and people, our experience of God has become shallow and empty, and thus we have lost what has been the very core of our heritage of faith. Our conversion to the cause of the poor and our dynamic participation in the struggle for justice will make it possible for us to know, once again, a rich, life-giving relationship with God and thus set us on a new journey of faith.

2. In this struggle, we will recover the richness of justification by faith as well as the revolutionary transformation of life that follows. When we realize the impact of the system from which we benefit on the poor of the world and accept our responsibility for its perpetuation, we will be prepared to explore, once again, what Luther discovered about forgiveness and justification. We will also know that this God calls, liberates, and empowers us to respond to this gift by giving our lives passionately in the struggle for justice. And as we learn to live by God's grace, we will help liberate those involved in the struggle for justice from an obsession with guilt and from a compulsion to justify themselves, problems that often hinder the liberation struggle.

3. As we witness the presence and power of the Holy Spirit in the Christian base communities and strive to form communities of faith in which poor and marginal people can claim their right to minister to each other, we will be able to appropriate for ourselves Luther's revolutionary discovery of the universal priesthood of all believers and draw from it for the radical restructuring of congregational life. What he perceived about the nature of Christian faith nearly five hundred years ago is capable of challenging our whole ecclesiastical structure, for he showed us that only a church in which those considered to be at the

<u>bottom are fully in charge of their common life can live out
the gospel that the church preaches.</u>

> "We are all equal by every right, and having cast off the
> yoke of tyranny, should know that he who is a Christian
> has Christ and that he who has Christ has all things that
> are Christ's and is able to do all things."[1]
>
> "[My aim is] to make the way easier for the unlearned—
> for only such do I serve."[2]

What does this say to us about the authority of laypersons, especially those who do not have university degrees?
Or about the superior authority, in the church, of scholars
who understand a theological language far removed from
the conceptual world of the people? Or about our failure to
allow women to share fully in the life and ministry of the
church or to honor their way of thinking and acting? "No
laws may by any right be laid upon Christians, whether
by men or angels, without their consent; for we are free
from all things." What <u>popes and bishops have done to
impose laws on Christians without their consent is tyranny.</u> "To be subjected to their statutes and tyrannical
laws is to be made the bondslaves of men."[3]

Does this challenge us to look more closely at how our
judicatories function and at the way our church life is
ordered from the top down? Or at our failure to create
conditions for the people to engage in dialogue with the
Bible and with our theological heritage, to be encouraged
to articulate their faith, and to order their common life?

> The works of monks and priests, be they ever so holy and
> arduous, differ no whit in the sight of God from the works
> of the rustic toiling in the field or the woman going about
> her household tasks.[4]

What might it mean for us, in the lives of our congrega-
tions, to give the same prestige and honor to the humblest
members that we give to those we recognize as leaders? Or
to structure our community life so that we give as much
attention to their spiritual and vocational formation as we
give to those aspiring to be pastors?

4. As we situate ourselves in the midst of the poor and allow our consciences to be stirred by their suffering, Luther's ethical stance will once again provide us with a compelling motivation for sacrificial service, for Luther taught us that the life of discipleship flows out of an overwhelming sense of gratitude. God forgives us, accepts us as justified, and fills our lives with grace. If we receive this gift and realize what it means for us, we can only respond by striving to love others as God loves us, by becoming a Christ to our neighbor. Thus the ethical life is not a matter of carrying a heavy burden, dutifully obeying rules or keeping laws laid upon us. It is, rather, a matter of joyfully sharing with others something of the riches we receive daily. Today, as we become more and more aware of how Jesus Christ lived and gave himself to the poor and marginal people of his time, we are able to realize that we participate in this flow of grace in the world as we follow his example. This, I believe, is the witness of many martyrs in Latin America today, a witness that could break through to us with new power as we reconnect with our Reformation heritage.

The Possible Contribution of the Reformation to the Christian Base Communities

This revitalization of our heritage is, in my judgment, important not only for our Protestant churches but also for other Christians and the liberation struggles in which they are involved. All that Luther and his followers achieved belongs to all of us; it is part of our common history, whatever our church affiliation. As those whose lives have been shaped most directly by this historical experience are able to re-create it in our time and situation, that heritage can be available to the whole church, thus helping it to be faithful to its calling to be the "first fruits" (Rom. 8:23) of a new age. I believe that this heritage can especially contribute to the development of the base communities of the poor in Latin America as well as to the efforts of others engaged in the struggle for justice who are striving to live their faith in community.

1. In my contacts with members of Christian base communities, I have been tremendously impressed by their sense of the closeness of God and of the presence of Christ in their daily lives. At the same time, I get the impression that those who are most active in the political arena often lose this sense of the divine presence. As a result, they lose touch with the spiritual reality that could orient and sustain them in their suffering and struggles; they also fail to respond to the spiritual anxieties and longings of many of their neighbors, who then turn to otherworldly sectarian movements that alienate them from the struggle for liberation.

In this situation, Luther's emphasis on centering religious life and piety in the dynamic experience of God's direct and gracious presence can contribute significantly to the struggle of the poor for life today by freeing us from bondage to anything that tends to obstruct this experience. Grace, as the divine assurance of the forgiveness of sin, clears the way for a richer and fuller relationship with God. It exposes the limitations of the medieval idea of grace as a supernatural substance with healing power, which depersonalizes it. Because we expect to receive grace primarily through confession and response to the Word, rather than by partaking in the seven sacraments or by saying the right words in the ritual, sacrament and liturgy make this divine reality more real and thus take on new meaning for us.

2. While affirming God's initiative in responding to the cry of the poor, liberation theology has rightly placed great emphasis on the human responsibility for liberation, an emphasis especially important for those women and men who have been taught that they are worth nothing and can do nothing and whose sense of the divine has helped to maintain them in this position. Thus, Gustavo Gutiérrez speaks of "man the master of his own destiny"[5] and declares that "man forges himself throughout his own life and throughout history."[6]

But Luther, and later John Calvin, insisted that it is precisely our trust in the ever-present initiative of a gracious God that enables us to take full responsibility for the transformation of the world. This is what frees us to act dynamically as we live in communion with this Source of life and grace and find that we can direct all of our energies toward the struggle for justice.

Receiving daily from this Source, we can continue to struggle against all odds without experiencing "burnout"; we take responsibility for cultivating the life of the Spirit without being unduly concerned about our spiritual state. And we continue the struggle whether our efforts are recognized or not, whether we are affirmed or criticized, whether we succeed or fail. As Luther put it, we need "take no account of gratitude or ingratitude, of praise or blame, of gain or loss. As our heavenly Father has in Christ freely come to our help, we also ought freely to help our neighbor through our body and its works."

Trusting daily in God's forgiveness, we risk making decisions and dare acting courageously; we also find ourselves compelled to look critically at what we have done and to admit our limitations and failures. Responding to the voice of conscience, we act as though everything depended on us. At the same time we trust that, in the providence of God, our humble efforts will point toward the reign of God and contribute to its coming.

3. Luther declared that all the benefits of the gospel are mediated to us through the church, a fallible human institution. As he understood it, medieval Catholicism had erred in claiming that, somehow, the finite had been transmuted into the divine. The human Christ was received in his divine nature; the historical relativity of the church was sanctified by its divine character; the material in the sacrament was filled with grace. Against this, Luther, with his complete confidence in the sovereignty of grace, insisted that all forms of grace are finite and point beyond themselves. The divine appears in the world through the humanity of Christ, through the historical

weakness of the church, and through the finite material of the sacrament.

God wills to make available all the benefits of Christ in and through a church that shares in the limitations and distortions of human existence. Consequently, every attempt by those in positions of power in the church to control the faithful is exposed as idolatry. The church can guarantee its faithfulness as the bearer of grace only as it recognizes its finite human condition and strives to transcend itself and its past achievements.

4. The Christian base communities have re-created the Pentecostal experience (see Acts 2 and 4) of the church-as-community, a community of men and women who, possessed by the Holy Spirit, find themselves called to live a new quality of life as they share their material possessions and together seek to continue the work of Christ in the world. If this revolutionary breakthrough is be sustained and is to provide the foundation for a new model of church, it will need to have a solid theological foundation.

Here, I believe, Luther and the Lutheran heritage have something to contribute to us all, for he perceived that the church—as a sacerdotal-sacramental institution of salvation, a structure through which grace was mediated via the sacraments—had no compelling reason to value community. In fact, what was most essential to the existence of the church was its hierarchy and its priesthood, not its people.

For Luther, however, the heart of the church was found in a community of equals. God's grace is directly available to all, and all who receive it, whatever their social class or position in the church, are in equal positions before God. Moreover, as recipients of grace, each person is closely bonded to the other. The grace offered by a God of love leads inevitably to people becoming Christs to each other, sharing in love and responsibility toward society. God's grace is known and received through the reading of the Bible and the preaching and hearing of the Word, both of which depend upon the existence of a community of equals. In fact this community, mediating grace, comes to occupy the position formerly occupied by the priest and the sacramental system. Since we all have been raised up to the position of priest, we all have equal responsibility to make this community a reality. And as this community is absolutely indispensable, it must be re-created in any situation in which this quality of life does not exist. On this foundation, members of Christian base communities know that they already possess something absolutely essential to the life of the church, something the hierarchical institution may be in danger of losing. They are thus free to dedicate their energies to living out their calling rather than to feeling obligated to justify their existence or to defend themselves when called into question by that institution.

3

The Bible:
Source of the Truth
That Sets Us Free

The spiritual revolution initiated by the Reformers presented them with a new problem, whose solution took them another major step on the road to liberation. Their experience of forgiveness and justification as a completely unmerited gift of God was such that they were convinced, beyond any doubt, that this message was the truth of the gospel. But how could they make and justify such a claim?

The answer soon became quite clear: This truth had broken through to them as they read the Bible. Their spiritual search led them toward the Bible; the more they concentrated their theological study on it, the richer their understanding of this message and the more compelling it became for them. As a consequence of this experience and their reflection on it, they brought the Bible once again into the center of the spiritual and ethical life of the believer and worked out a new understanding of biblical authority. Together, these two emphases contributed decisively to liberation in the modern world.

Ulrich Zwingli, the Swiss reformer, described his spiritual journey in these words: "When I was younger I gave myself overmuch to human teaching, like others of my day, and when about seven or eight years ago I undertook to devote myself entirely to the Scriptures I was always prevented by philosophy and theology. But eventually I came to the point where led by the Word and the Spirit of

God I saw the need to set aside all such things and to learn the doctrine of God direct from his own word."[1] And Martin Luther, when challenged by the highest church authorities, declared, "We are simply forced to fly for refuge to that solid rock of Scripture, and not to believe anything, no matter what, that speaks, commands, or does anything without this authority."

The fascinating thing about all this is that the Reformers did not start out by developing a doctrine of biblical authority, which then compelled them to take the Bible's message seriously. Rather, they were grasped by a truth that broke through to them as they read the Bible and thus discovered that it was the bearer of an authoritative word. The God of grace spoke to them through the Bible and thus established its authority. Through the written word, God spoke a living Word. As the Reformers responded to it, they were compelled to affirm the power of the Word, mediated by the Bible, to order all Christian thought and all aspects of life in the church and in the world. And as they lived this out, they knew with certainty the truth that sustained them in the face of persecution and death. Thus, the Bible became the supreme source of liberation, bringing men and women into direct contact with the Source of life and thus freeing them from bondage to all written words in precepts, doctrines, and even the literal text of the Bible itself.

As a result of this discovery, the Bible made a unique contribution to human liberation. As they studied it in community, women and men encountered a Source of life beyond themselves. And they came to realize that, connected with this Source, they experienced liberation rather than bondage. Life grounded in faith in a sovereign God was daily energized by this divine presence at the same time that life was set free from all human attempts to box it in. Moreover, the Bible made this experience possible for every believer and provided the foundation for the exercise of a new sense of personal responsibility in society as well as in the church. Here I want to focus on several dimensions of this revolution flowing directly from Bible-centered faith.

A New Word for a New Situation

As the Reformers read the Bible, they were grasped by a *new* Word that spoke directly to their situation. In and through reading the Bible, they discovered a living Word and came to realize that the gospel is always the good news of tomorrow, never of yesterday.

This perception followed quite naturally from the Reformers' discovery that the God of the Bible is a God present and active in history, a God who wills the redemption of the world. Through our reading of the Bible, we encounter the Christ who is present in our world, creating, judging, and redeeming, the Christ who calls disciples to participate in this same ongoing redemptive process. God, then, is always up to new things and giving new commands; faithful obedience is a matter of keeping up with such a God.

It is thus hardly surprising that the Reformers, reading and studying this written Word from the past, found that it turned their attention toward the future, opened new horizons for life and thought, and led them to risk facing the unknown. This Word heightened their discontent with what existed and set them free from bondage to the past. To their own surprise, they found themselves engaged in the work of creation, giving shape to things that had not existed before.

This is not something Luther or Calvin discussed in great detail, but it certainly is what they did. As the Bible spoke a new word to them in their situation and that Word had the power to orient thought and give life to those who responded to it, this same Word equipped them to draw on the wealth of their tradition to rearticulate their faith for their time. As a result, their work of re-creation not only drew extensively on the theological tradition but demonstrated that it could contribute most when it was reworked in this way. On this foundation Calvin, in his *Institutes of the Christian Religion,* proceeded to systematically reconstruct Christian doctrine as he drew on the Bible to rethink and rework the fundamental doctrines developed over fifteen hundred years of Christian history. In so doing, rather than undermining the influence of earlier theologians, he aroused new interest in their thought and set new terms for interaction with them, especially Augustine and other theologians of the first four centuries.

Unfortunately, church leaders and theologians in the religious institutions growing out of the Reformation soon forgot this. In fact, they so revered the writings of Luther and Calvin that it was impossible for their successors to continue the creative theological work these Reformers had begun. This produced theological stagnation, but the achievement of the founding Reformers was not entirely lost. Their witness has remained as a part of our history, reminding us of three things:

1. The greatest theological formulations, which provide the basis for faithful Christian witness in one historical moment, are necessarily limited by the culture out of which they emerge and the situation to which they respond. Only as the Bible mediates a living Word to us, which frees us from bondage to our past, are we able to transcend these limitations and speak as faithfully to our time as others have done to theirs. Through the presence of the Holy Spirit in a community, gathered around the Word while seeking to find the path of discipleship, this miracle happens time and again. As a result, we know that God is addressing us in and through a compelling new Word, and thus we need not depend, for certainty of faith, on old formulations guaranteed by a sacred text or by ecclesiastical authority.

2. The Reformation heritage carries with it a remarkable readiness to relate the Christian religion to historical conditions. This heritage also challenges the church to allow itself to be guided primarily by what it can become rather than by what it has been. The test of discipleship,

in the church as well as in the world, is our freedom to keep up with the God who goes before us.

3. This approach to the Bible allows us to see that Jesus began a life process that has continually transformed the world and that offers us the possibility of living transformation. Thus, faithful reading of the Bible, time and time again, leads to the formation of new groups around the memory of Jesus.

A Living Word

The Bible became a tremendous force for liberation because the Reformers insisted that, in and through this human word, God comes to us directly and addresses us personally. Jesus Christ, God incarnate, is the Supreme Word of God. Consequently, the Bible-as-text points beyond itself to a divine reality.

This affirmation is closely related to what Paul had to say about the God who chooses the path of self-emptying—coming to us in a poor and powerless person, Jesus of Nazareth—the God who does not overwhelm us by power but comes to us in weakness and humility. This is the God who speaks to us through human words and places upon us the responsibility to think, study, and strive to understand the Word within the words, as addressed to our unique situation. And because the Holy Spirit is present and active in and through the study of these words, we are freed from the temptation to control this revelation or to reduce God's Word to our limited thought and perspectives. As we no longer need to absolutize the written Word to find security, we can see any such attempt for what it really is: a lack of faith that undercuts rather than guarantees divine authority.

Jesus Christ is the Word; this is the crux of the matter. In the Bible, God meets us in that person. Luther spoke of the Bible as "the cradle in which Jesus Christ is laid." Christ is "the Lord of the Scripture," thus Luther could go so far as to urge the "authority of Christ against the authority of the Bible." And Calvin thought of Christ as the organizing principle of the entire Bible. Christ is thus present in and through this medium while at the same time transcending it. The Bible makes possible this divine-human encounter, freeing us from dependence on intermediaries or on any cumbersome ecclesiastical apparatus of salvation. We know we are being addressed by a Word from beyond to which we must respond, a Word that can never be confined by our limitations, our thoughts, or our systems. Within this perspective, it is important to affirm that the Word of God is not bound to the Bible; rather, the Bible is bound to the Word of God.

Unfortunately, when Protestantism has lost its spiritual vitality, it has tended to abandon this trust in the presence of the Spirit and has sought security in the "verbal inspiration" of the Bible; this tendency has been especially noticeable among the Reformed churches tracing their origins to Calvin. They, however, need to be reminded that Calvin, with all his emphasis upon the authority and centrality of the Bible, made it very clear that the Word grasps us only when it is "sealed by the inward testimony of the Holy Spirit", not because of proofs. "Those who strive to build up firm faith in Scripture through disputation," he declared, "are doing things backward," for the highest proof of scripture derives in general from the fact that God in person speaks in it.[2] "Those who wish to prove to unbelievers that Scripture is the Word of God are acting foolishly, for only by faith can this be known."[3]

The Holy Spirit, however, does not work magic. As the human word is read or preached and we listen, Christ meets us and we respond. Only in this way does the Bible have authority over us. In *Protestant Christianity,* John Dillenberger and Claude Welch speak of "the intrinsic and immediate authority of the Word of God which can come fully alive in the human spirit only as by the Holy Spirit this Word is received in the responsible decision of faith."[4] Thus, we can say that the Bible *becomes* the Word of God; our reading and understanding of the Bible is an

Event, something exciting that happens to us as the Holy Spirit breaks through to us by means of the written Word.

This frees us from the temptation to make an idol of the biblical text, an idol that we feel called on to defend but that ends up enslaving us. Rather, the study of the Bible becomes an adventure in freedom as we trust in a power beyond ourselves and receive a gift of new life. It is a rich personal and spiritual experience as Jesus Christ communicates himself to us; it is also an adventure in discipleship. As Calvin reminds us, we can understand the biblical Word only as we strive to live in obedience to the God who addresses us in and through that Word. When we follow this path, we come to realize that this type of Bible study happens in community and creates community. As we seek to understand God's revelation and dare to participate in the re-creation of the world, we find ourselves plunged into a communal experience of inspired living, which then opens our eyes to a richer understanding of the faith by which we live.

As those who rediscovered these dimensions of the biblical witness experienced its liberating power, they gradually came to three conclusions that had revolutionary consequences.

1. Their trust in God's self-revelation in and through the scriptures and in the presence of the Holy Spirit in the community gathered around the Bible freed future generations of Protestants to subject the biblical text to careful critical study, thus laying the foundation for modern biblical scholarship and all it has contributed.

2. Their discovery of the clarity with which the central message of the gospel broke through to those studying the Bible together led them to the realization that the Bible's message could be perceived by all and should be made available to all—thus the tremendous efforts to translate the Bible from Hebrew and Greek into the language of the people, to teach all the people to read, and to provide them with resources to carry on their own reading and study in the family and in the congregation. Before Luther, few

laypersons read the scriptures; Luther himself never saw a complete Bible until he was twenty years old. In 1522 Luther's translation of the New Testament appeared in German, and more than one hundred thousand copies of it were sold during his lifetime. And between 1520 and 1524, more religious pamphlets were published than at any other time in German history.

3. The Reformers realized that if Christ meets us in and through this biblical Word, offers us life, and calls us to respond, then this personal experience is essential for every Christian. No one can do this for another person. Moreover, each person, in order to be able to respond, must be free to hear and understand the Word in his own way. For Luther, this was so vitally important that he could declare that the Scriptures free men's consciences. Inevitably, this perception led to the affirmation and the defense of religious freedom and other freedoms essential for responsible living.

The Revitalization and Liberation of Theology

This recovery of the centrality of the Word of God, mediated through the Bible, led to the revitalization and liberation of theology. Reflection about Christian faith and its implications for life, in the language of the people, once again became an exciting adventure for laypersons as well as for pastors.

In the late Middle Ages, the theological enterprise was limited primarily to a small, specially trained elite who held positions of authority in the church. It was carried on in the realm of abstract conceptualization by means of rational argument, which only those highly trained in the use of such abstract processes could handle with ease. This rational development of theological concepts and their interconnection easily became an end in itself; the issues dealt with appeared to be far removed from the daily life-and-death struggles of the people.

The Reformers challenged such abstract thought at its

very foundation. If, in and through the Bible, Jesus Christ meets each person and challenges each person to respond, then each believer has the extraordinary opportunity and the tremendous responsibility to think about this biblical Word and come to understand what it means for herself and how it applies to daily life. Theological reflection articulates truth that orients, challenges, and transforms as it opens new perspectives on life and the world. To fulfill this function, such reflection must be a living and creative word. In this context theological reflection is, by its very nature, an experience of liberation that leads to liberation in other areas of thought as well.

Several elements in the stance of the Reformers contributed to this end. For Luther, the discovery that Jesus Christ was the center of the Bible meant that all theology had to focus on the soteriological question—"What must I do to be saved?"—that sets the agenda for systematic theology. Theology cannot be caught up in abstract and esoteric reasoning, far removed from the anguish and struggle of life. Theological reflection focuses on the person and the message of Christ, the redemptive process in history of which Jesus Christ is the center, and the human response to that redemptive process.

The Reformers also insisted that the Bible should be the supreme source of all theology and that the scriptures should serve as the basis for the formulation of all theological concepts. This, according to the distinguished German-American historian Wilhelm Pauck, represents their major contribution.

Calvin's *Institutes of the Christian Religion* became the classic model for this type of systematic theology. In this volume, almost every page is filled with references to the Old and New Testaments, and the validity of each doctrinal statement is dependent upon its faithfulness to the biblical witness. On this foundation, Calvin was able to articulate the Christian faith with clarity, simplicity, and power. Moreover, this theological reflection, thus grounded in the Bible, clearly dealt with life-and-death issues and was permeated with religious conviction and emotion. As a result, in the words of one modern scholar, the human word is elevated and vivified by God's word. For this reason, Calvin's *Institutes* made a major impact not only in the sixteenth century throughout Europe but also on the modern mind.

Luther, with his biblically centered faith and his conviction that every believer had to bear the responsibility of responding to God's offer of grace, perceived that theological reflection is an enterprise in which all believers can and should be engaged. He realized that the biblical story was the story of God's people; it did not belong to priests or to an intellectual elite. A story told by the people in their language, not in abstract and incomprehensible philosophical categories, the Bible contained a message directed to the unlearned, and Luther was determined to address them in his theology.

Luther's determination brought about a tremendous simplification of theology, but this simplification did not limit the Christian message or make it any less profound. Rather, it freed theology from its bondage to alien and outmoded concepts that blocked an understanding of the richness of meaning and depth of insight of biblical images, symbols, and stories and thus opened the way for more serious and more creative theological reflection. As Biblical language once again entered the thought world of the people, it opened new horizons for thought and for life.

For Calvin biblical truth, by its very nature, called for obedience. Moreover, for Calvin, "all right knowledge of God is born of obedience"[5] and calls for obedience. This meant that he, as a theologian, was compelled to concern himself about the well-being of the city in which he lived. In fact, his great ambition was nothing less than ordering all aspects of life of Geneva by the Word of God in the Bible.

Across the centuries, this emphasis on the right and responsibility of every believer to engage in theological reflection has also opened the door for developments of which the Reformers would not have approved. Individuals and groups have come up with theological formulations that depart from the central lines of the tradition and have tried to impose them on their churches or start new denominations. From time to time, the life of a church has been disrupted by one type or another of popular dogmatism or anti-intellectualism, which seeks to defend the faith by reducing it to a simplistic formula. And Protestant theologians have sometimes been caught up in the same sort of abstract academic games from which Luther and Calvin hoped to free the community of faith. But their witness remains a part of our history, capable of creating a space in which Christian folk in specific situations of struggle find themselves encouraged to take up the Bible, listen to its clear and compelling message, reflect upon it, and apply it to their lives—and thus bring new life to the church and new richness and depth to the theological enterprise.

A Self-Authenticating Word

Luther and Calvin found in the Bible a compelling Word, grounded in the sovereign and transcendent initiative of God, which no institution had the right to control. They thus found a new source of authority that freed them to hear and to respond to God's call—and to challenge the claims of any religious institution standing in the way of their response.

This was, of course, a very daring and risky business, especially given our human tendency to use biblical texts to justify and to validate our ideas and desires. This meant, for Calvin, that the biblical exegete, as well as every Christian, must make a determined effort to understand and listen to what any text really says. The Bible is a historical document dealing with historical realities. Only in treating it as such making use of those methods of analysis and interpretation that best contribute to that end, can it be understood.

For Calvin, the greatest enemy of such historical understanding was the allegorical (or "spiritual") method of interpretation, which allowed the interpreter to make a text say almost anything. Such a method particularly served the interests of the religious establishment by permitting church authorities to make the biblical text conform neatly with prevailing doctrine and practice. To counter this method, Calvin insisted on serious efforts to analyze what the text said and to allow it to speak on its own terms. And while he declared "that alone is true faith which the Holy Spirit seals in our hearts,"[6] he also made it clear that we must use the written Word to examine the Spirit.

When such efforts are made to discover what the biblical text is saying, we can trust the Spirit and can rest assured that God's Word will break through to us. Calvin declares that God is the author of scripture[7] and the biblical message is self-authenticating.[8] Consequently, there is no need to have the authority of the church certify the authority of scripture. Luther put it even more sharply: "What the church says is not the Word of God, but the Word of God says what the church will be. The church does not make the Word, but is made by the Word."[9]

This meant that the Bible was given the central place in the life of the church and of the believer. Freed from institutional control, the Bible became a means of constant renewal and revitalization of the church. At the same time, the Bible became a source of tremendous spiritual revitalization and ethical transformation in the lives of the people as believers read it daily, expecting to be addressed by God, and took on themselves the responsibility of responding to that Word. The church's control of the Bible domesticated the Word and held people in bondage; the Reformers' liberation of the Bible from such control, while affirming the authority of the Word over the individual believer and the church, opened the way for an experience of liberation that eventually affected other areas of thought and life.

4

The Bible,
the Protestant Heritage,
and Liberation Today

Over the centuries, the revolution that Protestantism started in relation to the Bible has gradually spent much of its force. To be sure, we continue to emphasize the centrality of the Bible in our worship and in our lives, put it in the hands of all believers, and urge them to read it. But much of its power to transform human life and to revitalize the church has been lost. I believe that a number of factors have contributed to this.

As Protestants have dared to live fully in the modern secular world and have been influenced by the spirit of the Enlightenment, they have often come to the conclusion that the biblical story, which speaks of a transcendent God intervening constantly in nature and history, belongs to a more "primitive" world in which they no longer feel at home. Thus, the Bible fails to speak to them in a compelling way. Moreover, as members of mainline Protestant churches have accepted uncritically the values and way of life of the middle class, they conceive of the gospel as a message having to do primarily with the spiritual growth and development of the individual Christian. As a result, their eyes are blinded to the radically subversive and transformative social message of the Bible.

On the other hand, fundamentalist Protestant groups have struggled to defend and to preserve the authority of the Bible and its place in the life of every Christian. But, in order to do this, they tend to emphasize the "verbal inspiration" of the biblical text and its "infallibility," thus giving divine authority to those texts that support their preferred dogmas. They often reduce the biblical message to a set of doctrines that dare not be questioned. In their zeal to defend the Bible as the Word of God, they may end up making an idol of it. Christian faith is reduced to rational statements, formulated in the past. As a result, the liberating power of the transcendent Word is largely lost. The believer is no longer free to respond creatively to the Creator Spirit as that Spirit moves in the world today. And in this new situation of bondage, the pastor tends to tell others what the Bible says rather than trust the Spirit moving in the midst of the community to lead its members to the truth.

During several decades earlier in this century, the theological movement known as neo-orthodoxy focused attention once again on the richness of the biblical witness and aroused the interest of many Protestant church people in Bible study. Unfortunately, such study tended to become academic and was often limited to small, elite groups. And those who participated in it by and large, did not find themselves compelled to live in solidarity with the victims of injustice and to read the Bible with them.

But while we Protestants have been struggling, without too much success, to preserve the authority of the Bible and to experience its power to transform our lives and our communities, an extraordinary and unexpected thing has been happening elsewhere. Groups of Roman Catholics, especially in Latin America, have directly experienced the authority and power of the Bible, just as the Reformers did, by doing today the equivalent of what was done in the sixteenth century. By this I mean that these latter-day reformers felt compelled, by their faith, to enter fully into the agonizing spiritual situation of their time and place: the horrendous suffering and oppression of the poor majorities in their countries. As they did this, the gospel broke through to them with a new and compelling message that they could not ignore. And this breakthrough occurred as they read the Bible and as the poor in the Christian base communities studied it and allowed it to speak to them.

As a result, something else occurred that was very similar to what happened in the sixteenth century. In and through this study of the Bible, women and men found themselves in the presence of God and addressed by God. As they responded, their lives were enriched and transformed. The Word created community, and those gathered around that Word were empowered to struggle for justice and to face persecution and death.

In this situation, the Bible has once again become the very center of Christian faith and life, a tremendous force for liberation, and once again those thus affected by the biblical Word have reestablished its authority. Or, to put it more correctly, the *Bible* has claimed its own place in the life of the church and of believers and has established its own authority. Its message is once again self-authenticating. The witness of the Holy Spirit confirms it in a way that no rational argument about infallibility possibly could.

In other words, Latin American Catholics are now making it possible for us to see more clearly what the Bible represented in the Protestant Reformation and how it can function in that same way for us today. If we are vitally in touch with our Reformation heritage and want to be faithful to it, then we should rejoice that this has happened. We should also take very seriously what it may be saying to us about how we can recover more of the richness of our heritage as a people of the Bible. Only as we enter into the depth of the human struggle of our time, as the Reformers did in theirs, and there find ourselves addressed by God as we read the Bible can we hope to experience once again the power of the Word. For us at this time, this means living in solidarity with the poor and marginalized and reading the Bible with them as we join them in their struggle for life.

As we follow this path, we too may find ourselves living

a New Reformation. Brazilian Protestant scholar Antonio Gouvêa Mendonça recently remarked that "It's possible ... that the Catholic Church, through the Christian Base Communities, can yet awaken the Protestant Churches from their stupor, and produce a new union of forces necessary for Christian action for renewal in our country and on the continent."[1] I share this hope, but I would express it somewhat differently. I believe that the awakening of conscience taking place among many Protestants in the face of the suffering of the poor and of the witness of the base communities is laying the foundation for a new engagement with the Bible. In fact, I already see this happening, especially among small groups of Pentecostals and other Evangelicals who are closest to the suffering of marginal people. As this happens, we can expect that our Protestant experience of more than four centuries of giving priority to the study of the Bible will equip us to make an important contribution. More specifically, I believe that we will be able to recover the four dynamic elements of the sixteenth century Reformation examined in the last chapter.

Hearing a New Message through the Witness of the Poor

As Protestant faith communities made up of the poor struggling for liberation together with those in solidarity with them come together around the Bible, the same thing that happened to the Reformers happens to us. We are astonished to discover that the Bible is speaking a *new* Word to us. We come to realize that the gospel is indeed the good news of tomorrow, not of yesterday. And we may be a bit surprised to discover that our study of the Bible over the years has prepared us to hear this Word, now that our ears have become attuned to it.

Several examples of this come to mind, related to my personal experience in recent years.

1. I find that when I study the Bible with poor and marginal people, texts I have known for years become the

bearers of a new message for me. This happens time and again as I read the Psalms, the writings of the Hebrew prophets, or the Gospels and become aware, as never before, of God's concern for the poor, God's justice, or Jesus' vision of the reign of God.

I see the same thing happening to others. I recall a series of Bible studies I did several years ago with a group of Pentecostal pastors in Chile. In one of them, we were reflecting on the Song of Mary, in the first chapter of Luke's Gospel, in which she speaks of God putting down the mighty from their thrones and exalting those of low degree, filling the hungry with good things, and sending the rich away empty (Luke 1: 52–53). In the course of the discussion, one pastor remarked, "Every year for more than twenty-five years I have read the Bible from cover to cover. But today is the first time I have really heard these words."

2. I have always been fascinated by the fact that, across the centuries, the reading of the Bible has led to the awakening of conscience as God has opened the eyes of men and women to human suffering and has called them to do something about it. In the past, this stirring of conscience often focused on the plight of those millions living and dying without Christ. Today, this same awakening of conscience is happening through the reading of the Bible but is more sharply focused on the horrendous suffering and untimely death of the poor and the oppressed. In each instance the Spirit, moving through the Word, calls men and women to service and to sacrifice. Time and again, that Word calls forth new responses in new historical situations, and, precisely in that way, Christian faith remains a dynamic reality.

3. In studying the book of Acts, I have been amazed to see how the Holy Spirit constantly calls the small community of faith formed after the resurrection of Jesus to face new situations and to respond in ways that go beyond anything they have done before. The disciples are still dreaming of the restoration of the Davidic kingdom; Jesus tells them to forget that dream and to become witnesses to

his suffering and victory (see Acts 1: 6–8). On the day of Pentecost, they are called to sell their possessions and live in community, having all things in common (2: 44–47). Before their own community is well established, the Spirit leads them to heal the sick, evangelize the people around them, and face persecution (chs. 3–4). Before they have developed fully their own church order, they are called upon to create a new order of deacons to minister to the needs of non-Jewish widows (Acts 6:1–6). Most revolutionary of all, the Spirit leads Peter to evangelize and baptize Cornelius, a Gentile, an action that went against what Jesus himself had done and had advised his disciples to do (chs. 10–11).

As the Holy Spirit moves in a similar way today, we may be helped to recover our Reformation heritage. We will realize that we witness to the authority of the Bible not by rational arguments in its defense but, rather, by our willingness to respond to the moving of the Spirit in our situation. In fact, we will realize that the most dramatic demonstration possible of the transcendent nature of the Word of God addressing us in the Bible is our freedom to give up the security of established patterns and to risk thinking new thoughts and envisioning new horizons. We will be most faithful to Luther, Calvin, and others who have shaped our past not when we repeat what they said and did but when we draw on their lives and thought to respond creatively to the challenges before us.

As long as we simply try to preserve that past—as expressed in theological concepts, forms of church organization, or patterns of discipleship—it easily becomes a burden, alienating us from our struggles today and limiting our responses. But when we strive, above all else, to respond to the leading of the Spirit in our time and place, we will be astonished to discover how those who have gone before us speak to us with new power and provide us with rich resources to be creative in our situation. Their achievements help us to do in our time what they did in theirs.

As we learn, once again, to trust the power of the

biblical Word to orient us toward the future and to open our eyes to God's dynamic presence in our history, we will realize that our Protestant experience over the centuries of living with the Bible can make an important contribution to the renewal of the church today, be it Catholic or Protestant. When we perceive how, time and time again, the Holy Spirit has led those reading the Bible to express their faith in new and compelling ways in response to specific human needs, we will be prepared to challenge all attempts, in the name of God, to stifle the Spirit. We will see how the leaders of any church, Catholic or Protestant, are tempted to seek security by giving absolute value to past achievements and to guarantee their own positions of prestige and power. And they do this by claiming that what they possess, in doctrine or church organization, is divinely established. But to the extent that the biblical Word is for us the good news of tomorrow, we will see that this longing for security closes the mind to the Word rather than honoring it, and replaces the creativity of the Spirit with a process of sclerosis, leading to spiritual death. Or to put it in other words, trust in the living God, speaking ever anew to us through the Bible, is replaced by idolatry.

At the same time, as we rediscover our history as a people compelled, time and again, to hear and respond to a new and strange Word addressed to us, we will be prepared to face and overcome another temptation frequently present in the community of faith. Precisely because the Word of God deals with the concrete realities of our day-to-day life in the world, we can become so caught up in those struggles that we pay little attention to the fact that we are addressed by a Word *from beyond ourselves*. Our immersion in the intense struggle for a more just society may distract our attention from the mystery of the divine and from the spiritual dimensions of life that originally inspired our struggle. When this has happened in our Protestant history, new communities have formed around the Bible that have recovered this experience and have challenged the church to give greater attention to it. This, I believe, is a major reason for the recent growth of charismatic movements and Pentecostal churches in both North and South America.

Jesus Christ: The Living Word in the Christian Base Communities

As the poor in the Christian base communities study the Bible and seek God's guidance in their struggle for life, the Bible once again speaks a living Word. Through it, God addresses them, and Jesus Christ moves among them. They become acutely aware of the presence and power of the Holy Spirit in their midst. To the extent that, in our Protestant faith communities, the poor and those who stand in solidarity with them gather around the Bible in this same spirit, this miracle happens once again, and our history of familiarity with the Bible comes alive in new ways.

For many Protestants, this affirmation may seem completely unwarranted. We believe that this experience of the Bible as the living Word is precisely what has been at the heart of our Protestant history. I know that this is our claim. But my experience of the vitality of Bible study in Christian base communities—in contrast to what I see so often in our own churches—has led me to the conclusion that something has gone wrong. As we have cut ourselves off from the struggle of the poor for justice where Jesus Christ is present in our world, we have lost contact with this dynamic spiritual reality. Lacking this assurance, we tend to seek security by making an idol of the text and defending a dogma about the authority of the Bible. Rather than trusting the movement of the Spirit in the community as it gathers around the Bible, we feel compelled to tell others what we are sure that the Bible says. Govêa Mendonça goes so far as to declare that "the Bible has lost its place in Protestantism and has been transformed into a secondary instrument used to justify ideological structures of thought which are frequently authoritarian, unjust and even evil."[2]

Only when we are willing to risk everything to stand with Christ in his struggle in the world will the experience of our founders come alive for us once again. Then our study of the Bible will bring us to a new awareness of the living Christ. The Bible will once again become the center of our life of faith and will manifest its own authority. And we will be empowered to understand and live what has been so central in our Protestant attitude toward the Bible. We will be free to accept it as a historical document, written by human beings, through whose witness the Holy Spirit addresses us. And we will trust the movement of that Spirit among the people rather than find ourselves compelled to try to control the Word through our teaching and preaching. We will know that the Bible is essentially a source of liberation. And, when we dare to follow Christ in his identification with the poor and marginal, we will be astonished by the richness and depth of what the Bible has to say to us.

On this foundation, we will also be prepared to make an important contribution to a New Reformation in Latin America and elsewhere. Our Protestant experience with the Bible, over the centuries, has prepared us to insist that the Bible, as the source of a living Word, frees and compels us to deal critically with the biblical text, giving full recognition to the way in which God speaks to us, through fallible human words, in and through the specific conditions of particular cultures and histories.

Consequently, we can be faithful to the Word only as we constantly make the effort to understand God's incarnation in Christ in the concrete situation of Palestine two thousand years ago and to discern what that incarnation means in the very different situation in which we live today. This is especially important when we are dealing with issues such as male-female relationships, which oblige us to take into account the ways in which the patriarchal society of Jesus' time blocked an awareness of the radical nature of the gospel and its implications for human relationships. When we face this imperative, our Protestant history of critically examining the Bible makes it possible for those reading the gospel from the perspective of the poor and marginal to hear and to respond to a Word directed to them today and also to experience once again the liberating power of that Word.

Theological Renewal in Dialogue with the Oppressed

When, in our communities of faith, the poor and those living in solidarity with them seek guidance in the Bible—and are surprised by a new encounter with Jesus Christ—our theology is transformed. Just as in the time of the Reformation, the Bible breaks the hold of abstract elitist theologies, far removed from the struggle of a suffering people for justice. Theology is, once again, simpler yet more profound and takes on a new life of its own in the world.

Two startling discoveries are at the center of this theological renewal. First, Jesus Christ, the One who lived and walked with the poor and marginal, took up their cause and centered his life and preaching on the advent of a new order of justice and equality, the reign of God, in which the poor would occupy the privileged position; for this he was crucified by those in positions of privilege and power. Second, those who today join him in this same struggle are called upon to share his sufferings and, at the same time, to find themselves sustained by the divine presence. In this context, theological reflection becomes, once again, an exciting adventure not just for an elite but for the people of God.

Just as in the sixteenth century, the theological task is sharply focused and is thus simplified and clarified. The good news proclaimed by Jesus is an offer of a full life, spiritual and material, for the individual person in the context of a transformed society, beginning here and now within history. The task of theology is to articulate and to clarify that message as it becomes a reality in the lives of struggling people. Theology thus must find expression in the language of the people in relation to the concrete situation in which they live, as it draws on and re-creates a long and rich tradition. A theology that names the reality of faith and hope by which people live not only focuses on what is most fundamental but also has a vitality and a depth not often found in more academic and abstract conceptualizations.

In this context, as was true for Calvin, truth is in order to goodness. Theology becomes a reflection of our struggle for life in relation to the struggle of Jesus. It is thought arising out of a response of faith that leads to a commitment to the poor in their struggle for life. It is part of a dynamic process in which thought and action are intimately intertwined.

Moreover, to the extent that we allow the Bible to set the terms for reflection, doing theology becomes a task for all believers, especially those who until now have had little opportunity to undertake it. The fact that the poor are the human authors of the Bible, that it has been produced by the poor or from the perspective of the poor—means, as Pablo Richard reminds us, that the poor are the "privileged interpreters of the Bible."[3] They are the persons whose social situation and experience best prepare them to understand its message. This means that the trained theologian is called on to put his knowledge and training at their service, to establish contact with them and their symbolic world, to honor their history and experience as well as their language, and to help them name their world of faith.

As this happens, the story of the people struggling today and the stories of the people in the Bible come together in an exciting way; the theology born of this encounter takes on new life and gives life to a wider circle of women and men. The Reformers encouraged the formation of a new community of faith in the home, as the family gathered daily around the Bible. As a result, they initiated a process of theological reflection that made the gospel come alive for the people and brought it to bear on daily life in the world. Today, we can re-create that experience in the natural, grass-roots communities of marginal, oppressed people and others committed to the struggle for justice and peace. As we do so, Christian faith will come to play a more important role in shaping thought and action.

The Self-Authenticating Word in the Struggle for Life

As the poor and those who stand in solidarity with them study the Bible and are grasped by the Word, they rediscover one of the most important elements in our Reformation heritage: the power of the Bible to establish its own authority. When Protestant communities involved in this struggle undergo a profound transformation, live joyfully and hopefully, and experience God's closeness in the midst of persecution and death threats, they know just as the Reformers did that the biblical Word is self-authenticating.

I'm convinced that only this compelling experience will make it possible for us to see how far we have departed from our Reformation heritage. Only in this way will we be able to see that, as our churches have lost the spiritual vitality that comes from participating in Jesus' struggle for the reign of God, we have become obsessed with a yearning for security—and have fallen into the same error of the medieval church that led to the Reformation. At that time, a spiritually decadent church tried to save itself by sacralizing the religious institution, thus making an idol of it and holding people in bondage to it. Today, a spiritually decadent Protestantism tries to save itself by sacralizing the text of the Bible, thus making an idol of it. And those who are most insecure tend to lash out against anyone who dares to expose this betrayal of our heritage.

However, when those committed to radical discipleship live by the power of the Word, they know that they are being addressed. Once again the Bible establishes its own authority. Convinced of its truth, we are no longer obsessed with trying desperately to find security by absolutizing the biblical text. And once again we experience the mystery of the freedom of the Word: Our confidence in the witness of the Holy Spirit, which frees us from bondage to the biblical text, compels us to do our utmost to understand that text, through which God addresses us. To do this today means, I believe, at least three things.

First, we Protestants must recognize how a distorted view of biblical authority frequently interferes with our serious study of the Bible. On the basis of his study of Brazilian Protestantism, Govêa Mendonça goes so far as to claim that "the schematic reading of the Bible has no need for exegetes and interpreters, those who know the original languages, in whom Protestantism took so much pride in the past. They are no longer necessary ... they are dangerous because they can destabilize, with their scholarly work, the established ideological/religious system."[4] Does this apply only to the present state of Protestantism in Brazil? Over the years that I have taught seminary students, I have been surprised by the frequency with which students, here as well as in Latin America, have refused to explore what a particular biblical text had to say because they feared that it might call into question their narrow worldview and thus threaten their security.

Second, we must realize the challenge that the study of the Bible in the church of the poor presents to biblical scholars as well. I have spent many years in academic institutions in which discussions of biblical authority have had a central place, but they rarely led to a conviction about the authority of the Word or to more faithful obedience. On the other hand, as I have taken part in Bible study in base communities, I have frequently been astonished by both the depth of insight into the meaning of the biblical story and the almost spontaneous response of those studying it to the message it contained. On such occasions, I have realized that they have done more to establish the authority of the Bible for me than semesters of academic study carried on in a context in which this willingness to hear and to respond was not given a central place.

Moreover, as one who tried for years without much success, to encourage young people and students to engage in Bible study, I'm aware of the fact that, as Robert Clyde Johnson has put it, "the vitality of Biblical studies in recent years has been almost fantastic; but those familiar with the situation will concede that with marked exceptions this expanding breadth and depth in the understanding of the Scriptures has caused hardly a ripple in the church."[5] I'm convinced that this failure can be overcome only as the biblical scholar carries on her work in the context of commitment to the struggle of Jesus and of a community dedicated to it.

Third, we are faithful today to the seriousness with which Calvin and other Reformers sought to discover what the biblical text really had to say only as we take into account the social and political context out of which the biblical narratives emerged. Poor and marginal people are able today to understand what the Bible says and to be convinced of its authority because they stand close to where the biblical writers stood, whether they were slaves in Egypt, prophets overwhelmed by the injustices around them, or disciples of Jesus living on the periphery of the Roman Empire. Their rereading of the scriptures challenges us to open our eyes to look critically at the ideological blinders we have used until now and to take the steps necessary to better perceive what the biblical writers have to say to us.

I am convinced that our faithfulness as Protestants to this part of our Reformation heritage will be of the greatest importance in the next decade or two, for I believe that many of those to whom the study of the Bible has brought a new richness of faith and a call to discipleship are going to find themselves facing increasing opposition from a religious institution attempting to impose its own authority over scripture. In this situation, Luther's clarion call to obedience to the Word of God in the Bible over every other voice of authority is as important now as it was nearly five hundred years ago. But we Protestants can make that witness only as we reread that

Word with poor and marginal people and allow it to reorder our worship, our doctrine, our life in community, and our witness in society. If we dare to do this, we may be surprised to find how much our history, rediscovered and re-created, can contribute to our own spiritual transformation as well as to ecumenical efforts to firmly establish the emerging church of the poor.

5

Ecclesia Reformata Semper Reformanda

The essence of Protestantism is not a doctrine but a way of being in the world, a new conception of what it means to be the church that has revolutionary implications for all institutions in society. Some churches in the Calvinist tradition have come to express it by means of a Latin phrase, *ecclesia reformata semper reformanda*. By it, they declare that any church that is a product of the Reformation deserves that name only as it is capable of overcoming the drive, inherent in all human institutions, toward self-preservation, and only as it dares to re-form itself, from time to time, in order to respond creatively to the challenge presented by new historical situations. Faithfulness to a living God, active in the world in order to transform it, calls for new responses on the part of an ever-renewed community of faith—in the words of John Milton, "the reforming of reformation itself." In its application to society, this concept is referred to as "the Protestant principle," which calls for the desacralization of all human achievements, institutions, and structures.

Wilhelm Pauck speaks of this principle as the heart of Protestantism, determining its dynamic character and thrust in the modern world:

> Protestants have always acknowledged that the concrete historical situation in which men find themselves is the

place where obedience is to be rendered to God, but, at the same time, their prophetic spirit has moved them to criticize, in the name of God, every attempt to render any historical attainment permanent and to regard it as sacred because of its alleged permanence. Thus, they have shown a great eagerness for religious reform whenever a historical tradition, particularly an ecclesiastical one, threatened to become an end in itself.[1]

As our Protestant churches have not distinguished themselves, in recent times, in their fidelity to this aspect of our heritage, I consider it important for us to look more closely at the origin and meaning of this discovery by the Reformers.

The clue to this revolutionary perspective is found in the answer Martin Luther and John Calvin discovered in the Bible to the question obsessing them: Who is God? Luther, as we have seen, met a God who comes to us directly, taking the initiative in offering us forgiveness, in justifying us, and in giving us the gift of life. Calvin came to know God, the great Creator and Redeemer, as a sovereign God, acting in history with a purpose, a God who calls men and women to share in this great drama of redemption. We can perhaps get a clearer idea of the radicality of their discovery if we consider that medieval Catholicism tended to conceive of God primarily in relation to space while Luther and Calvin understood God primarily in relation to time.

As I pointed out earlier, theologians strongly influenced by Greek thought tended to conceive of God as the Supreme Being, at the top of a great ladder, or chain, of being. The Creator God, who made every form and part of the universe, filled every vacant space, putting each thing or species—angels, human beings, animals, plants, and stones—in a precise place in this great chain. This created order was not only determined by God but was also by nature hierarchical; those orders farther down the ladder possessed less "being" and were thus inferior to those above. Moreover, each order had within it this same hierarchical arrangement.

Consequently, the established order of things in society possessed something of the divine and thus was not to be tampered with. A hierarchical structure of reality required that those in inferior positions recognize the authority of those above and treat them with reverence. And the church, given its unique position in this realm of Being, participated in a very special way in this divine reality, which gave even greater legitimacy to its hierarchical order. Within this realm of being, it was only natural for people to perceive signs of the presence of the divine almost everywhere, but it was difficult to experience a personal relationship with a personal God.

In and through his reading of the Bible, Calvin discovered and was grasped by a God who broke this chain of being and opened the way for a radical transformation of the church and the world. This God is the creator of all things, which belong to an order separate from God, a discovery that establishes a sharp discontinuity between the divine realm and all of creation. This God stands alone. Nothing created by God has any claim to divinity or any divine right to lord it over others. There are no intermediaries, persons who can claim divinely given status or power, whether it be angels or the Virgin Mary, popes or kings, bishops or feudal lords.

The Creator God, who neither needs nor tolerates intermediaries, is present and active in the world and in history as the Redeemer God. This God wills the transformation of the world and is ever active efficaciously to achieve it, standing in judgment on what now exists, bringing into existence new and unexpected things, and thus orienting human life toward the as yet unrealized future.

This God is also sovereign, above and beyond all our thoughts and systems and known only through the divine presence and action in history as perceived with the aid of revelation; thus, the divine will is the central reality undergirding and ordering the world. Over it we can have no control. God is present directly, acts directly, and exercises power directly in history—and calls us to find our place in this redemptive process.

In all of Calvin's writings, whether commentaries on the Bible or more systematic theological expositions, what comes through on every page is his tremendous sense of the closeness of God at all times, a God who can be seen and felt, a God who is involved in every moment and every aspect of our existence. And because this sovereign God is the God who takes the initiative in forgiving, justifying, and saving us, we can trust our lives and our destinies completely to God's care. As Calvin wrote, "what is more consonant with faith than to recognize that we are naked of all virtue, in order to be clothed by God? That we are empty of all good, to be filled by him? That we are slaves of sin, to be freed by him? Blind, to be illumined by him? Lame, to be made straight by him? Weak, to be sustained by him?"[2] And living daily by this grace, we are free to give our lives completely in grateful response: "We are God's; to him therefore let us live and die. We are God's, therefore let his wisdom and will preside in all our actions. We are God's; toward him, therefore as our only legitimate end, let every part of our lives be directed."[3]

But this God, who offers such complete security to the believer, guarantees no such security for the established order of church or society. On the contrary, as historian Michael Walzer puts it, Calvin's God "overthrew kingdoms at a stroke, sent churches into precipitous decline, waged war against rebellious angels, and bore the claims of no man—bishop or pope or king—to stand above his equals and to mediate between them and himself."[4]

This God acts in the world not through divine agents within a chain of being but through those who are directly called, with whom God makes a covenant. It is this call and command, rather than a given status or birth within society, that turns people into instruments of God's redemptive action. And as Calvin clearly perceived, these people are not usually those at the top or in the center but those at the margins, often unattached persons and wanderers free to respond to this call and to become pilgrims.

With this God as the ultimate point of reference and source of support, believers experienced a tremendous sense of liberation. Traditional authorities in church or state had no absolute claim upon them. All institutions could be subjected to radical questioning. And those who experienced this freedom could direct all their energies toward the transformation of the world in line with the divine purpose for it.

Applying This Theology to the Church

Given the fact that religion played such an important role in the lives of people in sixteenth-century Europe, the Calvinist Reformers gave primary attention to the implications of this experience of liberation in the religious realm. This meant, first of all, an important breakthrough in the Christian understanding of revelation: The self-revelation of this God is controlled by God alone, not by the church. Moreover, revelation is dynamic in character. A living God, who is revealed in and through the liberation of slaves at the time of the exodus, in the midst of Israel and the nations at the time of the prophets, and in the person of Jesus Christ, is also present in the believer and in the community of faith. Such revelation can never be fully captivated by written words or by static doctrines and must be rearticulated, time and time again, in new situations.

Inspired by this vision, Protestants took the initiative in investigating the historical context in which the books of the Bible were written and in applying methods of critical analysis in their examination of the text of the Bible. Paul Tillich spoke of this as an event that had no parallel in other religions. They undertook the same type of historical-critical study of Jesus of Nazareth, thus giving greater importance to the historical Jesus. And in the same spirit, they studied the historical evolution of all systems of doctrine and looked at them critically, thus creating space for new articulations of the faith.

But this faith in a sovereign God, dynamically active in history, had even more radical and more immediate implications in the realm of ecclesiology, implications first perceived by Luther and later worked out more systematically by Calvin.

1. A sovereign God who takes the initiative in forgiving and justifying sinners as well as in the whole process of redemption in history makes use of *human* instruments to offer grace to human beings and to transform the world. Grace is made available to us through the historical weakness of the church and through the material in the sacrament. Finite forms point to the divine. The God who transcends all that we have and do but is present in and through all this makes use of, but is not bound by, structures or patterns that have been created by human beings.

2. As an instrument of the divine purpose, the church is an *Event* as well as an institution. It is a community called together by the Word to respond to it. The church is thus constituted by the Word; it stands under the judgment of that Word at every moment and is truly the church only when it lives by that Word. Thus, while it cannot exist without external forms, it must not be bound by them. Institutional structures are necessary but are not of the essence of the church. If and when they are considered permanent or regarded as sacred, they block God's redemptive action in the world rather than participate in it.

3. If God is related to time more than to space, leading the world toward the goal of God's kingdom, then the church can be the church only as it keeps up with this redemptive process and is, in the words of Paul, the first fruits of the new age. The church fulfills its mission not when it occupies a special space in the center of society but when it points to new possibilities open to society at any particular moment. As Eugen Rosenstock-Huessy has put

it, "Luther changed the church from a neighbor in space to a prophet in time. The church was to be not a hundred steps from the palace or the town-hall, but a hundred hours or days or months ahead of what was transacted in either of those houses."[5]

A God who meets us in new situations and calls us to new ways of life can only be served by a church that looks forward rather than backward. Rather than striving always for self-preservation, the church can be the church only if it makes room from time to time for discontinuity, only as it time and again dies to its past and experiences resurrection. It is faithful to Jesus Christ only as it witnesses to God's redemptive action. In other words, the church lives by re-creation more than by repetition as it dares to make room for and to encourage prophetic criticism as well as to form new groups in response to new challenges. Without this spirit, Protestantism stands under the judgment of its own principle and loses its reason for existence.

The spiritual revolution that produced an *ecclesia reformata semper reformanda* has had a profound influence on Protestantism over the centuries. Unfortunately, however, Protestant churches, old or new, have rarely discovered how to make room for the operation of this principle within their structures. Ironically, the monastic orders in Roman Catholicism represent more of a structure within the life of the church for offering space for radical renewal than we have thus far developed in Protestantism. We have seen everywhere many movements of church renewal that have brought new life to the church. But, all too frequently, such movements have ended up losing their cutting edge as they have been co-opted by the church institution or have simply been wiped out when they were perceived as a threat to the established order.

On the other hand, the vitality of Protestantism's response to new situations has found expression in each new era in the formation of a wide variety of new denominations. By this means, Protestantism continues to be a dynamic force in history. But churches from which they have sprung have been free to continue, largely undisturbed, in their old ways. At the same time, new denominations lose contact with much of the rich historical experience of Christianity. The church is more and more fragmented, living in class and cultural ghettoes. One of the major challenges facing Protestantism today is how to explore ways of moving beyond this impasse by developing, within but on the margins of the institutional church, structures for constant reformation.

Applying the Protestant Principle to Society

When Protestants live out their heritage of faith, they inevitably become agents of social transformation and, in certain situations, find themselves compelled to assume a revolutionary stance. A dynamic people, called to respond to the God who is ahead of them and sustained by a community living according to the pattern of death and resurrection, cannot function in any other way. When they take seriously their own Protestant principle, two things happen.

First, they develop a special sensitivity to and find themselves called on to resist every attempt to sacralize—and therefore to consider free from criticism—any achievement of the past, any way of life, or any social structure. If, in the church, God makes use of human instruments to achieve God's ends, then the same must be true throughout society. No movement or party, social structure or economic system, can be identified with the reign of God. On the contrary, all of them are human creations that can easily lose their creative vision and become sclerotic or be used by those in positions of power and privilege to serve their own ends rather than those of the wider community. Given this reality, we serve them best and are most loyal to them when we take a critical attitude toward them and work for their transformation.

Moreover, a vital faith in God compels us to expose and to denounce vigorously every attempt to give, to any human achievement or institution, a character of permanence or to consider it sacred, beyond criticism or change. This is idolatry, which means nothing less that making a god out of our own system or way of life and then worshiping it. Such idolatry is an evil much worse than atheism, for it allows us to hide from the living God of justice while we defend unjust structures with religious fervor. For this reason, across the centuries the descendants of Calvin have often distinguished themselves by the stand they have taken against tyranny.

Second, the God whose redemptive action transforms the world is engaged in breaking down and overthrowing structures of injustice in order "to build and to plant" (Jer. 1:10). This is the God who "has put down the mighty from their thrones, and exalted those of low degree . . . filled the hungry with good things and the rich he has sent empty away" (Luke 1:52–53). This sovereign God stands above, desacralizes, and judges all human structures so that those that block the road to God's reign can be torn down, thus opening space for the creation of new ones. Consequently, Christian discipleship involves reading the signs of the times in order to discern where such transformation is called for and how to participate in it. And, as Calvin well perceived from his reading of the Hebrew prophets as well as from the Gospels, those who are free to see the hand of God and to respond to this call are usually those at the bottom or on the margins of society.

Thus, Calvin's faith in God and his understanding of the church led him to undertake, in Geneva, a total re-formation or re-creation of the church and to set about reordering all aspects of its life by the Word of God. The city gave protection and economic assistance to a large number of religious and political refugees, many of them poor and marginal people trying to escape persecution elsewhere in Europe. In his letter to King Francis I of France, which he included as a preface to his *Institutes of the Christian Religion,* Calvin spoke of these refugee people, including himself, as "mean and lowly little men . . . if you will, the offscouring and refuse of the world."[6]

And the seal used by many Calvinist groups was Moses' burning bush, in flames but not consumed, a direct reference to the flames of persecution burning all around them at that time. A century later, the English Puritans, descendants of Calvin, took the leadership in the Revolution of 1648. They were the first political leaders in the modern world, according to Michael Walzer, to develop an ideology, strategy, and discipline of revolution, "the first of those self-disciplined agents of social and political reconstruction who have appeared so frequently in modern history."[7]

Only on rare occasions have the sons and daughters of the Reformation given such dramatic expression to their faith in a sovereign God through resistance to tyranny or involvement in revolutionary struggles. But this same spiritual experience has oriented and nourished many who have dared to look at and to judge what *is* from the perspective of what *could be,* who have found themselves freed from bondage to the past in order to live for and to create a new world, thus breaking the process of stagnation that comes from repetition. And this spiritual awakening has produced women and men who have known that they were *called* to make their contributions toward the transformation of the world and who could dedicate their energies to it in hope, whether their particular efforts succeeded or failed. What else can flow from a religious faith that is centered in a rich experience of the presence of such a God, from an attitude of complete confidence in the future promised by God, and from an urgent sense of mission born of yearning and hope for a time when those denied access to a full life will no longer be deprived of it?

6

Toward the Reinvention
of the Church

If the vision of a reformed church always undergoing reformation is at the heart of the Reformation of the sixteenth century, then the Protestant churches most closely connected to it historically should find themselves in a position of unique opportunity today. For they have the good fortune to be connected with a spiritual and theological heritage capable of freeing them from bondage to past achievements, calling them to respond dynamically to new challenges, and providing them with the resources they need to undertake the reformation of all aspects of their institutional life. And as they live this way, they present a constant challenge to all institutions and social structures to respond to new realities in the same way and thus to be open to ongoing transformation.

This witness is, I believe, urgently needed today as we face the demands for national self-determination and a new international economic order coming from emerging third-world peoples, the problem posed by the rapid exhaustion of the world's natural resources and the imminent ecological crisis, the failure of our affluent society to respond to the needs of the growing number of marginal people within it, and our increasing awareness of the crisis of our traditional system of values. All these represent challenges that can be met only as we move beyond our achievements of the past—and the deadends toward which we are now moving—and dare to take on the task of re-creating society.

Yet, precisely when this is called for, our major institutions seem to be bankrupt, incapable of undertaking the one thing necessary for creative response. A community of faith, committed to this vision and living by it, could contribute a great deal to keeping hope alive and could play an important role in the struggle for a more human world.

Unfortunately, I see little evidence that our churches are capable of responding to this challenge. Institutional Protestantism seems to be suffering from the same malaise affecting the rest of society. Rather than witnessing to the possibility of ongoing reformation, it negates its own principle as it dedicates its major energies to self-preservation and becomes a victim of the stagnation and sclerosis that come from repetition. A tradition born in an explosion of creative energy is often used to block the reinvention of the church called for at this time.

During this century we have seen many movements of renewal, but they have not produced a New Reformation. Neo-orthodox theology helped us to rediscover and rearticulate the theology of Martin Luther and John Calvin, theology that sustained the struggle of European Christians against a new wave of barbarism earlier in this century. But these theologians were not capable of drawing on this rich heritage to speak a new and compelling word in response to new challenges rushing toward us from the future. That response has come from elsewhere: from black and feminist theologians in the United States, from Minjung theologians in Korea, and from liberation theologians in Latin America.

In a world in which poor and oppressed people—in the United States as well as in the third world—are emerging as new historical subjects and many young people are exploring new spiritual frontiers and seeking new values, our mainline churches tend to take refuge within their middle-class ghettos. There, those who would save the church by reaffirming and giving absolute value to the theology and the patterns of church life and mission developed in the past seem to be gaining the upper hand, thus restricting more and more the efforts of those seeking to respond to new challenges. Once again, dynamic movements of spiritual renewal are breaking away and establishing new denominations, thus cutting themselves off from direct contact with important elements of our Reformation heritage, and are allowing sclerotic institutions to continue as they are.

At the same time, the elements of the gospel and of the Reformation to which we referred in the last chapter are still a part of our heritage of faith. More than that, they are still a part of us, waiting to be reawakened. As a New Reformation leads to the reinvention of the church in the Christian base communities and elsewhere, our contact with and experience of this new life in community can open our eyes to this subversive heritage and encourage us to draw on it.

I have seen this happen on numerous occasions with North Americans who have gone to Latin America or elsewhere in the third world as well as among those who have been willing to expose themselves to the sufferings and struggles of marginal, oppressed people here at home. In contact with a new breed of Christians, they have often undergone a second conversion and have rediscovered elements of the biblical and Reformation heritages long buried below the surface. In the context of this interaction between a New Reformation today and a lost history of reformation, we may lay the foundation in our time for a new historical realization of the *ecclesia reformata semper reformanda,* a struggle that should focus attention on several issues.

Incorporating Reformation into the Structure of the Church

The Reformers of the sixteenth century envisioned an *ecclesia reformata semper reformanda* but failed to order the life of the churches they established in such a way that this could happen. Today, partly as a result of the impact of the Reformation on the modern world—and with the example provided by the Christian base communities—we are in a position to carry forward what they initiated.

As we become attuned to their vision, we can also see more clearly the picture of the church presented in the New Testament, which points in this same direction. Jesus himself moves directly toward the poor and marginal people, calls twelve disciples from among them to constitute a new Israel, and brings together a new community. He establishes as a norm of God's reign that anyone who seeks to save his life will lose it, while whoever loses his life will save it (see Luke 17:33). Paul speaks of the church as the body of Christ, called to follow the pattern of death and resurrection; he conceives of that community as the "first fruits" of the new age. And in the book of Acts, the Holy Spirit leads the church, time and again, to move to new frontiers, to respond to new challenges, and to so structure its life as to be free to keep up with the Spirit of innovation.

We also have before us the restructuring of the church taking place in the base communities. In them, a new spiritual reality has produced a new model of the church; new wine has demanded new wineskins. The presence and power of God manifested in the lives of poor and marginal people has led them to give expression to their communion with God and with each other in a new community of faith. As we and they discover that the struggle for justice can go forward only as we are willing to lose our lives in that struggle, we get a new sense of what it means to be the church. As we watch the church grow and witness to its Lord through failure and defeat, persecution and martyrdom, we see more clearly how the church is called to live in the world. And as we find the strength to live as pilgrims along this road, with no worldly security, we experience the freedom the church is offered to structure its life in conformity to the creative and innovative Spirit.

This presence and movement of the Spirit today among the poor, just as in the early church described in the book of Acts, demonstrates what it means for the church to organize its life in line with the Creator Spirit. It proves that alternative structures are not only possible but also offer the only way to overcome stagnation. It challenges the church as an institution to make room for such new life within its structures. It also compels us, out of loyalty to the church, to give priority to its reformation, from time to time, whether the institutional church wants it or not.

A church faithful to this Reformation heritage will, I believe, strive to incorporate a number of things into its life as an institution, including the following:

1. The recognition that the doctrine, the liturgy, and the order of the church can faithfully represent Jesus Christ only as they are re-created in response to new historical situations. When we give absolute value to any historical achievement in any of these areas, what was once a creative response to the moving of the Holy Spirit blocks the movement of that same Spirit today. A confession of faith that sustained Christians in a life-and-death struggle in former times gets in the way of a similar response to a new challenge. A liturgy that made Christ's presence very real in an Anglo, middle-class culture makes it difficult, if not impossible, for poor Hispanics to perceive Christ's presence in their midst. On the other hand, fragments of confessions, a peasant mass, or the new forms of ministry emerging in the Christian base communities continue the dynamic process by which the incarnate Christ is present in our history.

2. The importance of making room for, encouraging, and listening to prophetic voices. The people of Israel may have stoned their prophets, but they also recognized that God had given those prophets a place in their nation and honored this recognition by preserving their writings in the scriptures. Jesus of Nazareth situated himself firmly within that tradition, and the apostle Paul included prophecy among the gifts given by the Spirit to the community of faith as essential for its edification. Even medieval Catholicism made room, within its structure, for Francis of Assisi and other such prophetic voices. How

much more important it is, then, for a reformed church *semper reformanda* to recognize and support those who are called to be prophets. For whenever God is present in the conscience and the Spirit is moving in the church, those most faithful will look critically at what the church is and is doing, expose its conformity to the structures of this world, and challenge it to be transformed in order to point toward the coming reign of God.

3. A willingness on the part of the church to accept its true place in the world, standing in solidarity with poor and marginal people, not alongside those with power and privilege at the top. The vision and energy essential for reformation come from the moving of the Spirit among those at the bottom and on the margins, together with those among the privileged who change sides and join them. This means that we finally have a chance to free ourselves from the burden of the long Constantinian era and from the long period of acculturation of Christianity within the framework of Christendom. But we will be able to occupy this position of solidarity with those called to transform the church and the world only as we learn how to become a poor servant church, capable of living and growing without depending on the wealth, the salaries, and the professional status to which we have become accustomed. And when revolutionary movements triumph and set about building a new order, we must strive to resist the temptation to carve out a position of prestige and privilege for the progressive church, for we can be faithful to the cause of poor and oppressed people only as we stay close to them, stand with them, and have the freedom to speak and act on their behalf, even before those in power who claim to represent their interests.

4. The recognition that the institutional church can fulfill its calling to be *semper reformanda* only if its subversive memory of the gospel frequently produces new movements within it, movements that show the larger church what it is called to become but that are structured so that they have the freedom to live out a new quality of life in community. During this century we have witnessed

the flowering of renewal movements in mainline Protestantism, but these movements' contributions to the reformation of the church have not been very great. The Christian base communities are the places where a new model of church has emerged and has established itself, resisting all attempts of the hierarchy to co-opt it while, at the same time, remaining firmly within and loyal to the church and the tradition out of which it has come. The ability of Protestantism to respond to the challenges before it today may well depend, to no small degree, upon our willingness to give priority to the formation of similar communities that constitute a sort of alternative church or the *ecclesiola in ecclesia,* "the little church within the church."

5. The realization that today a church oriented toward and structured for ongoing reformation can become a reality only as Catholics and Protestants of diverse traditions discover how to work together ecumenically to achieve that end. The Catholic church of the poor in Latin America is now demonstrating, for all of us, what a New Reformation can be. At the same time, it is threatened by a hierarchy for which the idea of an *ecclesia reformata semper reformanda* is heretical. We Protestants are the bearers of a theological heritage that compels us to always seek to reform ourselves, but we are victims of a history and of ecclesiastical structures that deny such reformation.

At the same time, as we have seen, Protestants and Catholics responding to God's call to stand in solidarity with the poor and to give shape to a new community of faith on that frontier are living a new unity. In and through that experience, we are learning to support each other as we bring gifts out of our particular heritage for the building up of the community and, at the same time, receive gifts from the other. It may still be too early to know what institutional forms this new ecumenical reality will take, but we can live it and trust that the same Spirit that led Peter to baptize Cornelius and open the early church to the Gentiles will lead and surprise us today.

Reconnecting with the Source of New Life

In the sixteenth century, the motivation and the power for the reinvention of the church came from an overwhelming experience of God's grace, bringing forgiveness and new life to men and women facing a profound human crisis. The reformation we hope for today can happen only as it flows naturally out of this same Source.

Can we expect such an experience of the divine in our time? Here again, I believe that the theology of liberation and the Christian base communities present us with a clear answer. They not only affirm that it is possible but are living it and are also pointing the way to it for us as well.

In *God-walk,* Frederick Herzog refers to this contemporary experience of God as the discovery that God is deeply involved in human struggles, conflicts, and sufferings on the side of those at the bottom and is known there by those who join in God's struggle for their liberation.[1] Thus it is not surprising that the poor experience the closeness of God as they live by hope and find themselves sustained in their struggle, suffering, and persecution. Those who are not poor experience this God in their conscience as a claim laid upon them, as a call to participate in the justice struggle, and as an experience of forgiveness and of new life along this road. Jesus Christ becomes a reality in our lives as we join him where he is, among the outcasts, and share in his suffering and crucifixion for their cause. And the Holy Spirit is present with new power in the communities of faith that take shape in the midst of this struggle.

In a culture that confesses the absence of any experience of God, we find women and men who are captivated by a new sense of transcendence and of mystery. As Herzog suggests, they stand in awe before God's impoverishment, God incarnate in a carpenter, moving along the dusty roads of Galilee, living among outcasts, and taking up their defense to the point of getting killed. They are awed in the face of the joy, trust, and hope so evident in the life of the poorest, deprived of everything yet so full of life, persecuted and threatened with death yet speaking so naturally of the God who sustains them.

Out of the richness of this experience, people are speaking once again of faith and are demonstrating its power to orient and to sustain their lives, even in the face of death. This faith is not primarily assent to an idea but is, rather, trust in the authenticity of a new experience of transcendence as we accompany the poor and marginal in their struggle for justice—a wager that, as we live in solidarity with them, we are connected with the dynamics of history and are sharing in a movement toward the coming of God's reign in history. In the midst of suffering and crucifixion, we experience the power of God manifested in lowliness. And as those at the bottom respond to God's call, God is raising up a new instrument for achieving this goal.

Situating Ourselves on the Frontiers of the Spirit

The logic of Reformation faith compels and frees the church not only to be the instrument of God's transforming work in the world but also to discern and be present on the new frontiers to which the Spirit calls it at any time and place. In the sixteenth century, this meant focusing on the family; today, it means focusing on popular grassroots movements, especially among poor and marginal people.

As we have seen, confidence in a sovereign God who wills the redemption of the world led believers to turn their attention from the church to the world, to be the church *in the world,* and to concentrate their efforts at those places where, through God's providence, a unique opportunity was found for the renewal and transformation of human life.

Luther perceived that, in his time, this cutting edge of God's reign was to be found in the family. And he proceeded to close the church during the week and make the family the primary community of faith and the center of the religious life. Each family was transformed into a spiritual unit, whose members read the Bible together, sang hymns, and prayed at meals in their own tongue. The *pater familias,* the head of the family, became the priest in this new community as the sacrament of the Word was transplanted into every household. People who feared supernatural powers no longer had to go to the church to escape the demons; the family became the place where the demons were confronted and were overcome. And in this way the gospel penetrated into the daily life in new and exciting ways. In the words of modern historian Eugen Rosenstock-Huessy, "By breaking with the special sanctity of the visible church, Luther made room for the Christian spirit to work in house and workshop as it had never done before."[2]

Today, we stand on the threshold of a new era as poor and marginal people emerge as the new historical subject and as a new consciousness develops among those who decide to change sides and stand with them. In this situation, all sorts of popular or grass-roots movements are emerging and are rapidly coming to occupy a position similar to that of the family in sixteenth-century Europe. In them, people alienated from the dominant institutions and social structures are beginning to perceive their world in a new way. They are creating new patterns of relationships among themselves, envisioning new economic and political structures, and developing new strategies for social transformation. The success or failure of their efforts may go a long way toward determining the shape of their future as well as their participation it .

By means of the Christian base communities, a New Reformation is establishing itself in the center of this new world. In and through these communities, the gospel has been brought into the center of the daily life of the poor. Those formerly marginalized now discover their worth before God. Their faith enables them to cultivate a new quality of interpersonal relationships, to learn how to empower each other, and to organize themselves to struggle for their liberation. And in these communities of mutual empowerment, new ministers are recognized and trained for building up this new form of the little church within the church.

The vitality of these communities has been demonstrated not only by their rapid growth in some areas and by their contribution to the popular movements but also by the way they have sustained their members in times of persecution and in the face of brutal repression. The large number of martyrs in Guatemala, El Salvador, and elsewhere witnesses to the depth of their faith and the presence of the Holy Spirit in their midst. But their situation is also very precarious, especially in those places where they face opposition, if not persecution, from the hierarchy and violent repression from civil and military authorities.

They have shown an amazing ability to reinvent the church as they have discovered how to express their faith in their own words and develop new liturgies, give expression to that faith in music and song, and come up with new programs of action in their local communities as well as new forms of political engagement. But some of these new communities also demonstrate the stagnation that can come with repetition, as the experience of the founders is passed on to a new generation rather than re-created by them; as the liturgies, music, and confessions of faith arising out of a moment of spiritual vitality are repeated year after year; as patterns of community organization and programs of action become routine, are imposed on new situations, and thus block more creative responses; and as the excitement of the discovery of the gospel message of liberation gives way to the indoctrination of a new generation for whom that message will have vitality and power only as they are helped to discover it for themselves and articulate it for their situation.

Can the emerging church of the poor perceive this danger in time and discover how to be *semper reformanda?* I think this is possible, given the newness and the vitality of these communities, their relative freedom from the heavy burden of a frozen ecclesiastical tradition, and the fact that they are essentially base communities. That is, they have been energized by the new sense of subjecthood of the poor and marginal and recognize the importance of the revitalization that comes from below.

I also am convinced that the heritage of the Reformation can make an important contribution toward this end because of its doctrine of God, its understanding of the church, its emphasis upon the prophetic vocation, its concern for ongoing transformation, and its capacity, time and again, to produce renewal movements. But we Protestants must realize that this heritage will be present as a dynamic spiritual force only to the extent that we are present in the struggles of poor and marginal peoples and in the popular movements, only if we are as captivated by this new frontier of the Spirit as Luther was by his sense of the importance of the family in his time, and only if we are as committed as he was to shaping a new community of faith where women and men are struggling for life in the world.

By now it should be clear to us that our mainline Protestant churches are not and will not be present on this frontier to any significant degree. The Protestant presence will be expressed primarily through Pentecostal churches and other churches that are identified with the poor and have the potential of becoming churches *of* the poor. Those of us who are, historically, most closely connected with the heritage of the Reformation must realize that it will significantly affect the poor and their popular movements today as is taken seriously and appropriated by these "younger" Protestant churches.

If we realize this, then we should be much more concerned about making resources available to these churches than about the missionary extension of our middle-class churches into the world of the poor. In a number of countries in Latin America, scholars, pastors, and lay leaders from Lutheran, Methodist, and Presbyterian churches are finding a variety of ways to do this, especially in theological education and other forms of leadership training. The time has come, I believe, for us to explore a wider range of possibilities for such collaboration here in North America as well.

Reinventing the Church Where We Are

The spiritual renewal taking place among the poor, their witness to the transformative power of the gospel, and their spirit of hopefulness and joyfulness in the face of tremendous suffering and persecution have profoundly affected many of us in positions of relative privilege who have had contact with them. As a result we often find ourselves, somewhat to our surprise, embarked on a journey that may lead to *our* spiritual renewal as well.

Through them we hear a cry to which we know we must respond. An imperative has been laid upon us from which we cannot escape. We know we must become involved in peace and justice struggles, in solidarity with those who are suffering and dying, to challenge the system that benefits us while depriving them of food and housing, education and medical care, and the opportunities to be employed and to occupy positions of worth in society.

And as we turn to our religious heritage, we realize that this imperative, communicated to our consciences through the poor, is not just some vague sense of moral obligation but a call from God. We find ourselves *addressed;* we realize that God is meeting us in and through those who suffer. In responding to their cry, we enter into a new relationship with Jesus Christ and find ourselves captivated by Christ's passion for the coming of God's reign. In my conversations with priests and lay women and men in Latin America who have given up a life of comfort and professional careers and are daily risking their lives because of their commitment to the struggle for justice, I've often been struck by the fact that they don't speak of this in terms of a moral obligation. At some point, their consciences were disturbed by the suffering and death around them. But in and through their response to the cry of those marginalized and crushed by a system of injustice, they have experienced what they often refer to as the closeness of God.

As our faith and commitment grow, we are confronted with major questions we had not faced before: how to understand what is happening around us in the light of our biblical faith; how to look critically at our system of values and our way of life as privileged middle-class people; how to work for any real transformation of our society and its structures; how to continue the struggle when we see little or no progress toward our goal; and how to deal with criticism, opposition, and possible persecution when we strive to respond to these challenges.

We soon realize that we cannot deal with these issues *Where?* individually; we must do so in community. But the church as we know it, with its present membership and program, is concerned about other things. Its worship as well as its theology rarely equips us for this struggle. If we want to explore such questions from a faith perspective, we will have to do so with others who have a similar commitment to the struggle for peace and justice today and know that they urgently need the help and support of others. In other words, the reinvention of the church is as important for us at this moment as it is for the poor; we must find the equivalent of the Christian base communities in our own situation of struggle.

These communities emerged as the result of years of struggle on the part of a few people who had been captivated by a vision of what a church of the poor could be and who kept working at the formation of such a community until a breakthrough occurred. An equivalent of these communities may emerge among us as small groups of those whose faith has led them into the struggle for justice for poor and marginal people come together in a similar way. As we discover how to create a new quality of life in community, while drawing on and living out our faith, we will also be engaged in the reinvention of the church and will demonstrate, once again, what it means to be an *ecclesia reformata semper reformanda*.

Thus far, we have no blueprints for such communities. We do know that there are many people who yearn for this experience and who are interested in working at this task.

As we take it up and learn from each other, we know that we can count on the Holy Spirit to lead us. In the next two chapters, I will explore what the Radical Reformation of the sixteenth century may be able to contribute toward this end.

Keeping Alive the Belief that Society Can Be Transformed

Communities of faith living the heritage of the Reformation keep alive, throughout society, the belief that transformation is possible and maintain a dynamic witness to it wherever they find themselves. Their faith in a sovereign God makes them sensitive to all attempts to ascribe a sacred character to human achievements, especially when they stand under divine judgement. Inspired by a messianic vision of a more human and a more just world, they are compelled to take a prophetic stance against any unjust status quo. And the death and resurrection of Jesus Christ has established a pattern by which we can move toward a fuller life, individually and collectively, as we are free to die to our past, break out of deadends producing stagnation and decay, and allow new possibilities of life awaiting us on the other side to surprise us.

This witness is crucially important for us in the United States at the present time as people around the world are getting a new sense of their own identity and strength, are dreaming of a new world, and are discovering how to work together to create it. As a result, third-world peoples are striving for ethnic and national self-determination, thus challenging the domination of all superpowers. Third-world peoples are calling for a new economic order that will take seriously the needs of the poor majority. Those who have been deprived for centuries of the basic necessities of life yearn for economic well-being and, at the same time, have no illusions about the benefits of a market economy that focuses on the production and consumption of more and more commodities. As oppressed people come together in all sorts of popular movements for change, they are laying a new foundation for nonviolent change and for a more participatory democratic society; at the same time, the failure of the dominant elite to respond to these new aspirations will inevitably lead to violent repression and widespread social instability.

In such a moment, pregnant with exciting possibilities for moving toward a more just and a more human world, those in positions of power and privilege in the United States seem incapable of responding to this challenge. Instead, they have become victims of complacency and even of triumphalism, as they observe the deepening economic and political crises in communist societies and the apparently invincible strength of the global economic order of which we are a part.

At the same time, they are very much affected by the underlying malaise and gnawing sense of insecurity that permeate our society. But this awareness, thus far at least, has led them not to raise serious, critical questions about the status quo but, rather, to defend it by sacralizing it—or, to use a biblical term, by making an idol of it. In this way, all that is being called into question by popular movements at home and abroad can be affirmed uncritically, and those who dare to raise critical questions can be denounced as unpatriotic.

In this situation, those of us who are spiritually grounded in the heritage of the Reformation have an extraordinary opportunity and responsibility, for we live by a faith capable of exposing this idolatry for what it is, a faith calling for prophetic denunciation of injustice and, at the same time, offering a vision of a world transformed in the direction of the reign of God. We can envision a new future for our nation as we discover how to support the struggle of poor and marginal people at home and abroad for a new international order, for an economic system attentive to the needs of all, and for a new quality of life in local communities as people learn how to work together to meet more of their needs and empower each other.

But this can happen only as the heritage of an *ecclesia*

reformata semper reformanda leads to the formation of small communities dedicated to the reinvention of the church. Only in such intentional communities can we discover how to draw on our biblical and theological heritage to orient and sustain us in such a struggle, as we follow the way of the cross, and how to trust in resurrection and new life and thus sustain a dynamic witness to the possibilities for social transformation.

This witness is also needed today among those who are struggling for liberation, because radical social movements as well as efforts at national reconstruction can easily become victims of a frozen ideology or structure and can suffer from the stagnation that comes from repetition. Revolutionary movements, by their very nature, are oriented toward the creation of a world that does not yet exist. They appeal to women and men who dream of a different future and who are willing to give their energies and their lives to the task of inventing it. They grow as they appeal to others who dare to dream and who are willing to risk everything as they explore new paths and create alternative structures.

But the demands of this struggle also encourage those leading it to absolutize their ideology and their program, to discourage criticism, and to pass on and even impose their vision, as well as their achievements, on others. Those who once risked their lives in a struggle to create a new order and welcomed the challenge of a new situation every day can easily get caught up in bureaucratic routine. Others join them who have never had this experience of the founders or the creative vision that went with it. Early on, those in positions of power and privilege learn to enjoy these benefits, and seek to preserve them, while distancing themselves more and more from the grass-roots communities with which they were once associated. Eventually, a new generation of those who had no part in the original revolutionary struggle comes along and takes for granted its achievements and the contribution it has made to their lives. They, too, become victims of routine without any compelling cause for which to live and, when asked to make sacrifices, see little reason for doing so. And all too often those in power, instead of finding ways to challenge each new generation to dream of a new order and to take initiatives in the struggle for it, tend to rely on propaganda and indoctrination.

As the struggle to create a new political and economic order intensifies over the next decades in North America as well as in the third world, we have every reason to believe that Christian participation in these struggles will not only continue but will increase. If we take the heritage of the Reformation seriously, we will realize that an important element in our witness is the constant challenge to revolutionary movements to re-create themselves in order to stay alive, respond to new situations, and thus remain faithful to their vision and objectives.

This witness can be made only as Christians engaged in the struggle for liberation are sustained by communities that draw on the resources provided by the Reformation to orient their thought and action and also discover how to incorporate a process of constant reformation into their corporate life. As Catholics, mainline Protestants, and the churches present and growing in poor communities work together at this formidable task, the heritage of the Reformation may contribute to the formation of a church capable of transcending the historical limitations of Protestantism.

7

The Challenge
of the Radical Reformers

Any attempt today to reconnect with the Reformation of the sixteenth century must take into account those now known as Radical Reformers, who sparked a dynamic movement first persecuted and later ignored by both Roman Catholics and mainline Protestants. This extraordinary group of men and women discovered, through their study of the Bible, that God not only was directly accessible to them and offered them forgiveness and grace but also called them to follow the path of radical discipleship indicated by Jesus Christ. In this sense, they gave a new expression to a vision of the Christian life that emerged in Italy in the twelfth and thirteenth centuries with the Waldensians and in Moravia in the fifteenth century with John Huss and his followers: a call to make the gospel the guiding principle of life, giving special attention to the Sermon on the Mount; the conviction that Jesus Christ is the Lord of the world and that the social order should be shaped by this lordship; and a strong eschatological sense, focusing on the future transformation of the world. And both movements were led by men who were close to the poor, and whose message appealed primarily to them.

In sixteenth-century Europe, the spiritual journeys of most of these Radical Reformers were profoundly influenced by the preaching and teaching of either Martin Luther in Germany or Ulrich Zwingli in Switzerland. But their spiritual awakening and study of the Bible led them to look more critically at the established order of church and society, to seek a more radical transformation of both, and to criticize and eventually to break with their mentors. As their movement grew and spread, they were violently persecuted by both Catholics and Protestants, and their communities were almost wiped out. Known as Anabaptists because of their insistence on the rebaptism of adults, they survived in the Mennonite churches and the Church of the Brethren, and their heritage was passed on, somewhat indirectly, in the Baptist churches. Yet their vision and their way of life have had a profound influence on all our churches and continue to challenge us to this day.

As someone who has not been brought up in this tradition, I cannot explore it as part of my own history. I am, regardless of my attraction to it, something of an outsider, and I cannot hope to capture and express the richness of its heritage. But what I want to do here is to describe what the witness of this people has contributed over the centuries and what I consider to be its potential contribution to us at this juncture in history.

These reformers, just like Luther and John Calvin, were persons who, at some point in their lives, struggled with profound spiritual questions and were disturbed by the state of the church and of society and by the suffering of the poor, especially the peasants. Quite a few of them were priests or monks; the majority of the early leaders came from the upper class or from the emerging middle class. Conrad Grebel was the son of a member of the Great Council of Zurich and Thomas Münzer was a priest who had enough money to purchase seventy-five books at one time in order to pursue his spiritual quest. Luther or Zwingli had put most of them in touch with a gracious God and opened a new world of faith. Guided by them, they were able to take the Bible rather than the church as their ultimate source of authority. They embraced the idea of the priesthood of all believers and came to confide in the presence and power of the Holy Spirit in the community of

faith. For a number of them, their new experience of
Christ, mediated through the Gospels and the Pauline
epistles, led them to draw further on the medieval mystical tradition, with its emphasis on the presence of this
Christ in daily life and the importance of identification
with Christ. This meant that a profound evangelical and
mystical experience of encounter with Christ led them to
desire, above all else, to be completely "yielded" to Christ,
becoming like him and living as he lived.

For those having this experience, one thing sooner or
later became absolutely clear: Those who come to know
this Christ are compelled to follow him in all aspects of
their lives. Faith must lead to a total commitment to
discipleship, a passion for which comes not only from this
fundamental spiritual experience but also from an apocalyptic expectation, the conviction that this Christ is
bringing into existence the reign of God, which means
nothing less than the total transformation of the world.

As a result, these Reformers were not as much interested in working out the right doctrines about Christ as
they were in making what he taught and the way he lived
the basis for human life in the world. As reformer Ulrich
Stadler declared, the ordinances of Christ "should constitute the polity for the whole world."[1] For a few of them,
this meant taking up the struggle by means of social and
political revolution, but their primary concern was the
creation of a community of faith in which God's will for the
whole of humankind might be realized. Even Münzer, who
eventually chose the path of revolution, called for a
"renewed apostolic church," which would be a "mirror"
reflecting the advent of the reign of God. For him the
Reformation had as its goal the elimination of all evil in
the world, particularly the old ecclesiastical and feudal
social and political orders.

On this road, the closer they came to the Christ of the
Gospels, the more aware the Radical Reformers were of
the striking contrast between the way of Christ and the
reality of corruption, greed, and oppression in the society
around them—and in the church. And the closer they

came to this Christ, the more aware they were of the poor and the more they were drawn to them. As they came in contact with peasants, miners, and weavers and gathered them in small groups to read and study the Bible, they soon discovered that these poor were the ones who not only heard its message but were willing to take it seriously and put it into practice, which was often not the case with those more privileged who were fearful of what they might lose.

The Source of Corruption: The Church-State Alliance

How could the church, which conceived of itself as nothing less than the body of Christ, have departed so far from what it was called to be? For these Reformers, the answer was found in the close relationship that had existed between church and state from the time of Constantine. Thus they were led to attack the basic structure of church-state relations, the idea of the *Corpus Christianum* ("Christian Society"), by which the church allied itself with imperial power and shared in its exercise and in its privileges. Church and state were closely identified. All members of society belonged to the church, and the church legitimated and sanctified the existing social and political orders. In fact, these two orders worked hand in hand to maintain peace and order. Church and empire, pope and emperor, bishop and king, priest and nobleman shared responsibility for and saw themselves collaborating in the construction and defense of a Christian society.

For the Radical Reformers, this alliance had disastrous consequences. Because of it, the civil rulers as well as the clergy were blinded to the sad state of affairs, the reality of what Münzer called "poor, ailing, devastated Christendom."[2] They thus failed to realize that it was nothing more than an order "matted together with mud,"[3] incapable of holding together much longer. This so-called Christian society oppressed the poor, who already understood much better than their rulers what was happening and were turning against it. It also maintained a structure in which priests and monks not only abandoned their prophetic mission in order to flatter rulers and gain favors at court but also shared in the exercise of power and in the exploitation of the poor.

Given this structural reality, these Reformers concluded that there was simply no way to bring about a reformation of the church as long as this alliance remained intact. The gospel could shape human life in the world only if the church was separated from the world-as-it-is, which meant breaking with the assumption that people naturally belong to both of these realms. Anyone reading the Bible should be able to perceive that there exist two radically different realms, living by two different rules: the state, with its structure of power and privilege, and the church, a community of faith living by the norms of the coming reign of God.

Luther and Zwingli had initiated a movement that had opened the eyes of these Radical Reformers to the riches of the gospel, had deepened their faith, and had given them a new vision of the church. But somehow they failed to realize that the message they preached must lead inevitably to a break with the *Corpus Christianum*. By maintaining this church-state alliance, they could only end up providing a new religious legitimation for this sick and unjust society and failing in their efforts to reform the church. Thus the Radical Reformers were profoundly disillusioned with their mentors when they failed to follow through on the reformation they had started and instead began to persecute those of their followers who did.

The Essential Step toward Reformation: The Baptism of Adults

In their attempt to break with this identification of church with society, the Radical Reformers decided that the crucial issue was baptism. The baptism of infants was the way by which all persons in Christendom were included in the church; it was at the very heart of the integration of the two orders. Therefore, the reformation of the church would have to begin with the rejection of infant baptism. Only adults who were converted to Christ and committed to living as his disciples should be baptized. Baptism would then signify what it had in the early church: that such converts had died to sin and were now walking in newness of life. It marked their entrance into a community that lived by the norms of the coming reign of God and that was structured accordingly.

Soon, in and around Zurich and in those parts of Germany affected by Luther's teaching, those in the forefront of this movement were rebaptized and began to bring together farmers, miners, weavers, and others in small groups similar to the Christian base communities of recent times. In these small communities, they engaged in Bible study and prayer, read the words of institution of the Lord's Supper, and proceeded to share bread and wine. As they experienced the presence and power of the Holy Spirit in their lives, they struggled together to understand and to follow the teachings and example of Jesus and to allow their vision of the new age to shape their community life.

For these groups of humble people, their newfound faith awakened in them a tremendous yearning for liberation from the domination and oppression of the existing order, together with the conviction that God was mightily present in their midst to make such liberation a reality. For those influenced by Münzer and a few others like him, this meant that God had commissioned them to overthrow the existing order and bring in a new society, by revolutionary violence if necessary. Others, known as the Spirituals, conceived of a new order so radically different that they could come up with no institutional form for it, either in the church or in the society. Others, gathered together by Jacob Hutter and later known as the Hutterites, were determined to express the reality of the new age in communities that lived and worked together and practiced complete sharing of all material things. But the majority of those who were identified as Anabaptists, who faced persecution and possible martyrdom because of their faith, were dedicated to forming small communities which might make the reign of God a reality in history as they become the incarnation of suffering love. God's reign is essentially a new structure of relationships of giving and receiving, a new quality of life that can be developed only in community. It is thus a new way of living in and relating to the world and is so different from the norms of this world that it can only be worked out and sustained in community as a new church gathered around the Lord's Supper, the supreme expression of this new order of love and peace.

Captivated by this vision of the New Testament church and the coming millenial age, these Reformers were compelled to set about shaping this new community of faith and redefining its place in society. They realized that they had to define their faith theologically against the systems of doctrine worked out by the great doctors of the church and to restructure the church against the great ecclesiastical institution of Christendom. And they had to undertake all this while on the run, persecuted by Catholics and Protestants, fleeing for their lives without any sure place of refuge in the whole Holy Roman Empire, as one of them put it.

As Sebastian Franck wrote in 1531 to John Campanus, a Lutheran who had been converted to the Anabaptist perspective, "All that we have learned since childhood from the papists, we must all of a sudden again unlearn. Again, the same for what we have received from Luther and Zwingli—all must be abandoned and altered."[4] In their attempt to create a new order without models to guide them and without much help from the great theologians, some of them came up with exotic ideas; their passion for purity often led to narrow-mindedness and sharp divisions. At the same time, guided by the scriptures and by the Holy Spirit, they made important discoveries that were later taken over by mainline churches and that gave expression to elements of discipleship and qualities of Christian life in community that have challenged all of us to be more faithful.

The Transformative Power of the Anabaptist Vision

Among the contributions made by the Anabaptists over the centuries to the world church, I would emphasize the following.

1. The separation of church and state. The Anabaptists firmly established the fact that committed Christians are citizens of another world. The state is the realm of power and domination; the church, a community of love and service. The function of the church in society is not to legitimate these structures of power but to be a prophetic voice, exposing their injustice and corruption. The church is not oriented toward the high and mighty and the conquest of prestige and power but toward the poor and marginal people of the world and an effort to raise them up. Never completely at home in this world, it lives "in the wilderness," a pilgrim people witnessing to the future reign of God.

2. The church as a community of believers. Because of the radical character of the gospel, those who hear it are called to repent, abandon their former way of life, and choose to live as disciples of Jesus Christ; thus adult baptism, symbolizing this decision to die to the old and enter a new sphere of existence, becomes centrally important, as does the demand that the church be a community, a believers' church, made up of men and women who have made a clear personal decision to follow this new way. As a result, the Anabaptists were the first to give priority to the evangelization of those within Christendom as well as those outside the Christian fold.

3. The local congregation as a community of shared responsibility. Luther proclaimed the universal priesthood of all believers, a concept the Radical Reformers were determined to practice. This meant, for them, that all believers must have the opportunity to understand the faith, to communicate it, and to occupy a position of responsibility in the community. But for this to happen, the role of the minister would have to be radically redefined as that of a servant rather than someone with authority over others. The early Protestant Reformers may have wanted to make this shift. But the Anabaptists perceived that, as long as the pastor was ordained in the old way, had control of the sacraments, and occupied a privileged position in society, he would be looked up to and would maintain his position of dominance. Only as the pastor became a servant of a persecuted community would it be possible to reorder congregational life so that all members could take responsibility. As a symbol of this new reality of community, footwashing was given prominence, to remind the community of the equality of all and the call to servanthood.

4. Christian discipleship involves sharing material possessions and responding to the needs of others. The Radical Reformers took seriously what Jesus taught about this as well as the sharing of possessions of the early Christians reported in the book of Acts (see Acts 2; 4). Calvin emphasized complete submission to the will of God in a life centered not in self but in service to others. The Anabaptists declared, by word and by example, that such service meant literally sharing material possessions with others. In fact, they perceived that sharing in the life of Jesus Christ calls into question the very idea of ownership, that a sharp distinction between "mine" and "thine" disrupts the body of Christ.

This concept was stated most categorically by Stadler:

> We learn it in Christ to lose oneself in the service of the saints, to be and become poor and to suffer want, if only

another may be served, and further, to put aside all goods and chattels, to throw them away in order that they may be distributed to the needy and the impoverished. That is the highest part and degree of divine abandon and voluntary surrender to the Lord and to his people through the Spirit of grace.[5]

Not all Anabaptists went this far, but this concern was present in all groups; some applicants for baptism were asked whether they would devote all their possessions to the service of the brotherhood and would not fail any members in need, if necessity required it and if they were able to render aid.

5. Vital Christian faith leads to nonconformity and is thus a subversive force in society. The early Anabaptists refused to take oaths, which were a means of ensuring political loyalty. They refused to go to war. Not caught up in acquiring property or gaining wealth, their spirit of sharing created a new economic model for both church and society. Denouncing injustice and the exploitation of the poor at a time of great unrest among peasants, they were easily seen as seditious. Living an ethic of love and nonresistance, they challenged Christians, in solidarity with Christ and the oppressed, to take up the cross rather than the sword.

6. The cross is central in Christian life; discipleship leads to suffering. Out of their experience of persecution, Anabaptists came to realize that following Christ leads to suffering with Christ. More than this, they perceived that such suffering makes an important contribution to the transformation of life and of the world and leads Christians into a more dynamic participation in the divine redemptive process. Some of them spoke of "the bitter Christ" they came to know, as opposed to "the sinful sweet Christ" of Christians living contentedly in Christendom. In the words of modern Anabaptist scholar Laverne A. Rutschman, "All agreed that discipleship involves taking up the cross of Jesus, a sharing of his suffering and not merely following his example or suffering on his behalf. They understood their suffering to be *with* him, a redemptive act."[6] This led them to conclude that "the follower of Jesus not only takes an option for the poor but is also called to share the suffering of Christ who is found in those who are helpless and defenseless."[7] It also led them to see how, in the Old Testament, God used tribulation as a means by which to bring God's people back to the path of service and obedience, as they were exiled in Babylon and then brought back to their land.

7. **"To know Christ is to follow him in life."**[8] These words of Hans Denck capture an insight that came to the Anabaptists when they realized that the majority of theologians in the centers of academic learning neither understood the truth they had discovered nor risked living by it. For Menno Simons, Christian truth had little to do with "subtly invented syllogisms or with any clever sophistries."[9] It is to be known in the midst of life, on the road to discipleship. The scriptures present the life and words of Jesus Christ and the apostles, not clever theological ideas. In a pamphlet entitled *The Mystery of Baptism,* John Hut declared that "no one can attain to the truth unless he follows in the footsteps of Christ and his elect in the school of tribulation."[10] And, if we want to understand, he urges us to "look to the poor, those who are despised by the world and called visionaries and devils according to the example of Christ and the apostles." This small community of believers, reading the Bible together, hearing *and obeying* the clear word of Christ, and remaining open to the guidance of the Holy Spirit, was in the best position to know the truth. In this context, theological reflection became the work of all, thus enabling every believer to communicate the gospel.

Those who were guided by this vision and who lived by these norms were rightly seen as dangerous subversives. Roman Catholics, Lutherans, and Calvinists were well aware of the fact that the spread of these ideas would lead to the disintegration of the established order of church and state. Consequently, the Anabaptists were brutally suppressed, especially in Germany, where the Reformation first launched a liberation movement that spread across Europe. In fact, the persecution was so severe that they were almost wiped out. And yet what the Anabaptists stood for, as outlined above, gradually had a profound influence on mainline churches, which eventually incorporated a number of these elements into their own faith and life.

And, despite the fact that these movements did not produce great works of systematic theology, one of their most important contributions, perhaps the most important one, was in the theological realm. As we pointed out earlier, the power of the Reformation lay in its radical reinterpretation of the nature of God and of God's redemptive action in the world. Calvin especially, with his emphasis on the sovereignty of God, centered faith in a God present and dynamically active in history for the transformation of the world.

This faith led directly to the Puritans' participation in the English Revolution of 1648 and enabled Calvinists to take the lead in breaking the hold of established orders of power and privilege, thus opening the way for new developments in industry and commerce as well as in parliamentary democracy. But the facile identification of mainline Protestantism with patterns of church-state relations worked out in the sixteenth century kept these churches from applying the Protestant principle to bourgeois society and thus from being involved in the frontiers of the justice struggle concerning capitalism.

In this historical context, the Radical Reformers made a unique contribution. By looking at both the apostolic past and the apocalyptic future and by rejecting outright the Christendom concept, they opened the way for new interpretations of history. They paved the way for the development of new theological perspectives on history within the Christian community and contributed to liberal philosophies of progress and to the historical views of

Marxism. As Howard Bender, a contemporary Anabaptist scholar, puts it, "the Brethren did believe that Jesus intended that the Kingdom of God should be set up in the midst of earth, here and now, and this they proposed to do forthwith."[11]

Their vision of God's rule over the world, their renewed emphasis on the writings of the Hebrew prophets, their interest in medieval millennial movements, and their total repudiation of the established order as sacred led some Anabaptists to focus attention on the coming reign of God and to interpret what was happening in history in relation to its advent. Münzer expressed this most dramatically in his preaching about the imminent establishment of the Fifth Age of Christ and the Third Age of the Holy Spirit. Others used different language to emphasize their expectation of a new era of social righteousness under the direct rule of Christ.

The eagerness with which they went about ordering the lives of their communities in line with the teachings of Jesus and the testimony of thousands of martyrs witnessed to the power of this expectation in their lives. And this contribution was destined to affect the church and the modern world even when many Anabaptist communities, struggling for survival in the midst of severe persecution, lost this vision of history and were more concerned about preserving the past than pointing to the new age breaking in from the future.

8

Toward a Radical
Reformation Today

What does it mean for us today to recover this lost history and to enter into a serious dialogue with the life and witness of these men and women who chose the path of radical discipleship and were sorely persecuted and often martyred? As I mentioned earlier, much of what they discerned and lived more than four centuries ago—the idea of the separation of church and state, the church as a community of believers, the emphasis on the initiative and responsibility of lay persons in the local congregation, and the recognition that following Christ calls for some degree of nonconformity—has now become an integral part of the theology and way of life of other Christian communities.

Moreover, by taking seriously what the New Testament taught about the coming reign of God and by daring to live by its norms, their witness not only exposed the injustices of the society around them but also pointed toward alternatives to the status quo. By rejecting private gain as the motivating force in economic life and by practicing the sharing of material things, they created a new model for economic life. They gave a new value to the labor performed on the farm and in the shop by insisting that priests and scholars do their share of it. At a time when the majority of men and women in Europe were illiterate, they set up excellent school systems and made education compulsory. And their opposition to war, coupled with their emphasis upon nonviolence as a way of life, has not only led other Christians to take New Testament ethical teaching more seriously but has also provided orientation and motivation for a much wider circle of people working for peace and for social transformation.

At the same time, while the churches connected historically with this Reformation have done an admirable job of preserving this heritage, there is one fundamental difference between the Radical Reformers and their present-day descendants. Anabaptists today do not, by and large, constitute a subversive force threatening the foundations of the established order. When those who participated in this movement in the sixteenth century decided to follow the teachings and example of Jesus and to live by the Sermon on the Mount, they were almost immediately accused of subverting the existing social order. In fact, their way of life was seen as such a threat that they had to be eliminated. In the German province of Swabia, one thousand men were hired at one time to hunt them down. So widespread was this persecution that Conrad Grebel could declare, "True Christian believers are sheep among wolves, sheep for the slaughter; they must be baptized in anguish and affliction, tribulation, persecution, suffering, and death."[1]

Why is it that the descendants of these Reformers, committed to this way of life today, are not usually considered equally subversive? It is possible, of course, that our world today is more open to and responds more positively to their radical witness. But I believe there is another, a more basic, reason for this difference. The Radical Reformers were acutely aware of where they believed the lines were being drawn, in their time, between the inbreaking reign of God and the kingdoms of this world. They were acutely aware of the structures of oppression and exploitation around them and challenged them directly. They experienced the Holy Spirit present in their midst as the Spirit of innovation calling for new responses on the part of a community of believers.

But the Anabaptist churches, just like the other churches emerging from the Reformation, soon fell into the routine of repeating earlier responses, thus preserving rather than re-creating their radical heritage. For some, this led to the preservation of specific elements of this witness while gradually accepting more and more of the values and life-style of the world in which they were living. For others, it meant a determined effort to preserve a way of life developed in response to sixteenth-century realities and thus become, to a certain extent at least, bound to the past rather than witnessing to the reign of God impacting us from the future.

While this is happening in Anabaptist circles, other Christians are, once again, discovering the radial message of the gospel for their time and place and are living it out. And as they do so, they are considered subversive and are being persecuted and killed, often in large numbers. Wherever new communities of faith take shape among the poor and those who stand in solidarity with them, among the victims of racism and sexism, or elsewhere in the struggle for peace and justice today, the experience and witness of the Radical Reformers is re-created in our time. And when you and I dare to listen to their witness and participate in such a community of faith, we may better understand what they said and did and may find ourselves drawing on it to deepen our faith and to orient our struggle today.

Standing today in a situation similar to that in which they stood, we too may experience a new awakening of conscience in the face of the horrendous exploitation and suffering around us, produced in large part by the global economic system from which we profit. In communion with them, our ears may become more attuned to the radical message of the Sermon on the Mount and its call to discipleship.

We may perceive more clearly the extent to which our

churches are at home in the established order of privilege
and power and are thus largely incapable of leading their
members along the path of discipleship. And we will
become increasingly impatient with bishops, pastors, and
theologians who are aware of all this, who may even speak
about their spiritual renewal, but who are not willing to
follow through on the radical implications of the gospel
that call into question their own comfortable positions.

powerful

We will be deeply moved by the manifestations of the
presence of God and by the power of the Spirit in these
new communities of faith, as well as by their willingness
to remain faithful when they are denounced as subversive
and persecuted and thus manifest a new quality of life
over against "the whole world," to use the words of the
early Reformers.

On this frontier of the Spirit in our time, the central
elements of the Radical Reformation of which we spoke in
the previous chapter may speak with new power to us.

The Separation of Church and State
and the Church of the Poor

The struggle for the separation of church and state
continues in our time when the church becomes a church
of the poor and orders its life by the gospel over against
the established order of exploitation and domination.

The Anabaptists declared that the church should follow
the path of Christ, even if this meant breaking with
nearly fifteen hundred years of history and culture.
Grebel insisted, along with Ulrich Zwingli, that the Word
of God, rather than the decisions of the Great Council of
Zurich, should determine the shape of the Mass and the
structure of the church. When the church today identifies
itself with the poor and marginal, it faces a similar
choice—whether to find its life and structure its community around service to those in need and the struggle to
transform society or to fit into and provide legitimation
for the present order of privilege and power. The Radical
Reformers constantly remind us that this choice can and

must be made. But we who are pastors, priests, or theologians face that choice today when we are compelled to decide between pursuing professional advancement in middle-class society or paying the price of identifying with and working for the empowerment of the dispossessed.

In sixteenth-century Europe, the baptism of infants was the supreme symbol of the integration of church and state; thus, for the Anabaptists, the rebaptism of adults was the decisive act by which the two realms were separated. As George Blaurock put it at the time of his rebaptism, "therewith began the separation from the world and its evil works."[2] But for us today, it is not by the baptism of adults but by the refusal to live by the rules of upward mobility and professional advancement that we draw a sharp line of separation between the two realms.

The Believers' Church and the Base Communities

Today the *idea* of the believers' church is widely accepted. But the reality of that church, as the Radical Reformers conceived of it, will be lived as we give shape to Christian base communities of the poor and to small faith communities made up of those committed to the struggle for peace and justice.

Luther realized early on that the majority of the members of his new church did not take seriously the demands of Christian discipleship. For a time, he considered forming a different type of church, made up of "earnest Christians" meeting separately from the mass of nominal Christians, but for some reason he dropped the plan. The Radical Reformers, on the other hand, were convinced that only such communities should constitute the church, even though such an approach would mean a sharp reduction in its size. In the words of Grebel, "It is much better that a few be rightly taught through the Word of God, believing and walking aright in virtues and practices, than that many believe falsely and deceitfully through adulterated doctrine."[3]

In the Anabaptists' effort to understand the wide gap between the New Testament picture of the church and the reality they knew, as well as the numerous examples in history of the "reconstruction of the ruined church," they came to the conclusion that the story of God's people is the history of *two* churches. In fact, for some of them, this history of two churches began in heaven, with the falling away among the angels, and continued with Adam and Eve, the people of Israel, and in the church, beginning during the apostolic era. God's struggle with the church is, time and time again, the history of the judgment, scattering, and restoration of the people of God.

remnant theology

By insisting on a small church of believers, the early Anabaptists were not calling for a community of those who had merely said they had faith in Christ or, as we would put it today, had made a personal decision for Jesus Christ. For the Lutherans and the followers of Zwingli, this profession of faith was the all-important criterion. By calling for a church made up only of believers, what was at stake for the Radical Reformers was discipleship: following Jesus by living according to a set of values and a life-style sharply contrasting with those of the society of their time.

In our time emphasis on conversion, on a personal decision, and on baptism as an adult by no means guarantees this type of discipleship. In fact, all these things often serve to reaffirm our middle-class values and our dreams of upward mobility and to tie men and women more closely to the dominant order of exploitation. And merely being a member of a Mennonite, Brethren or other church made up of direct descendants of these Anabaptists no longer subverts the established order.

his answer

If we want to take the Anabaptist vision seriously, we should seek to re-create the believers' church among poor and marginal people struggling for liberation along with those living in solidarity with them. For it is in such communities that identification with Christ and the experience of his presence among the sort of people with whom he walked in Galilee leads to radical discipleship.

Among these people, conversion to Christ means joining Christ in the justice struggle, and baptism means baptism into the suffering that comes from following the crucified One along that path.

The Radical Reformers broke with Luther and Zwingli when they realized that an institution at home in the *Corpus Christianum* could not sustain those committed to this way of life or become a community of faith for them. Those who had made the break with the values and norms of society and with the church integrated into it had to join together to reinvent the church, to give shape to a new community, a community in which a new experience of God and a new life of discipleship would provide a context for rereading the Bible, rethinking the faith, restructuring the liturgy, redefining spirituality, and reshaping relationships in community, a community capable of sustaining men and women as they strove to put the gospel into practice and faced persecution and martyrdom for it.

The Christian base communities have demonstrated that the same thing can and must happen today when poor and marginal people and those living in solidarity with them seek to articulate and express their faith. And their faithfulness to their vision and their ability to survive may depend upon their ability to rework all these elements in order to have a full ecclesial life.

A Church of Equals and a Community of Mutual Empowerment

For the Anabaptists, all members of the local congregation were called to take a full share of responsibility for its life; the pastor was not the one in charge of the flock but was the servant of a persecuted community. If we want to see where that concept is being lived out today, however, we must turn not to our mainline Protestant churches, or even to the descendants of the Anabaptists, but to the base communities of the poor. They are the ones who have recaptured the Pauline vision of the church, in which each member has a special gift (*charisma*) for building up the body of Christ, a church of equals learning to empower each other, where this rich diversity of gifts for ministry is recognized and each member is trained and is given an opportunity to serve. And if specially trained, perhaps ordained, persons are present, their task is to do everything possible to create conditions for the recognition and the exercise of these ministries.

The Radical Reformers realized that, as long as the pastor continued to exercise power and have authority as preacher of the Word, congregational life would focus on him and on a small elite gathered around him. And his presence would be an obstacle to the realization of this goal. But over the centuries, congregational life among Anabaptist descendants has tended to become more like that of mainline churches rather than that of their original vision. Moreover, in the sixteenth century, the Anabaptists perceived that, to be faithful to this vision, their communities would have to provide an alternative to the structure of power dominant in the *Corpus Christianum*. What they have not perceived so clearly today is that, in faithfulness to their heritage, they ought now to radically challenge the structure of domination at the heart of our liberal, middle-class society. Throughout our society, institutions are organized around the principle of boundary management (or "the turf"), autonomous zones of jurisdiction whose members are committed to maintaining, defending, and extending their realms.

At the center of this system are middle-class professionals, persons who have been specially trained to solve problems and provide services for others in the particular area in which they are experts. Their personal identity, and sense of importance and worth, are defined by their positions within that structure. Moreover, their success is measured by their ability to be upwardly mobile, which means not only to improve their economic positions but to occupy positions of greater prestige in the community and to influence a larger number of people. The result is that the more successful they are, the more they deprive others of the opportunity to take responsibility for their lives and thus become Subjects. The minister or pastor is part of this world, with its values and goals, and functions the same way. Moreover, he is generally more concerned about winning the acceptance and approval of his congregation and advancing professionally than with providing a clear prophetic witness.

too often true!

Only as this professional mentality and structure is overcome can the local congregation be faithful to its calling. The Christian base communities have demonstrated that this can be done and that, as it happens, the church once again becomes a subversive force pointing to the transformation of the world in the direction of God's reign. In such a community, footwashing might recover its original meaning and power.

The Sharing of Material Possessions

The Anabaptists not only declared that Christian discipleship involves responding to the needs of others and sharing material possessions but have kept this witness alive in the Christian world across the centuries. Ever since Jacob Hutter gathered together a group of starving and homeless refugees from religious persecution to organize the first Bruderhof in Moravia, these communities have practiced a complete sharing of material possessions for more than four hundred and fifty years. Today one hundred and ten such communities, with more than ten thousand members in the United States and Canada, continue to live that way. Moreover, the Anabaptists continue to remind us that Christian love cannot be authentic if it does not include this material dimension and that the spiritual life of committed Christians must deal daily with the demon of obsession with possessions and must lead directly to sharing material things.

Where is this pattern of Christian life being followed today? I do not see it happening in our Protestant churches, whatever their denominational origin, but I have found it in base communities of the poorest people. Among those who have nothing, the Holy Spirit is present as it was in the early church and leads to this type of sharing, even of the last kilo of rice or of the little one-room shacks in which they live. A Catholic sister working in a slum in Recife, Brazil, tells of a conversation she had with a woman living there: "God came to my house today," said the woman. "I didn't have the money to pay for medicine for my son, who's sick. My neighbor earned money doing laundry for the whole week. It was one hundred *cruzeiros,* and she gave it all to me to buy medicine. That could only be God, don't you think?"[4]

This witness of the base communities and our recovery of this dimension of our Protestant heritage could help us to hear once again the call to discipleship and to explore ways of expressing it as we give shape to a believers' church appropriate for our time.

Nonconformity

From the beginning, the Anabaptists claimed that following Jesus Christ meant nonconformity, and they have practiced this from one generation to the next as they have adopted a simple life-style, often lived apart in their own largely rural communities, and refused to take part in war.

But as they and those influenced by them follow this pattern today, they are not being denounced and repressed as dangerous subversives. In the sixteenth century, their nonconformity challenged the ideology and structures of domination of their time. Their Christian faith and their way of life put them clearly on the side of the peasants and the lower classes in the new cities in an explosive situation of great social unrest. And their frontal attack on Christendom was seen as something that would ultimately destroy the existing order in Switzerland and in Germany.

Why does this same way of life not have the same impact today? The answer is not hard to find. The early Anabaptists' orientation toward the future, based on their trust in the dynamic action of God in history to establish

God's reign, led them to attack the roots of injustice in their society and to envision radical alternatives to it. But today the repetition of what they did does not usually put men and women of faith at the cutting edge of the struggle for justice.

The roots of injustice in our society are found in the alliance between the wealthy, powerful elite in each country and a global economic system, the most fundamental challenge to which is coming from the emerging popular movements. To the extent that Christians challenge this system of exploitation and participate in the development of alternatives to it, in the political as well as economic realms, their nonconformity becomes as subversive as the Anabaptists' in the sixteenth century.

For this reason, I believe that the Christian base communities should be recognized as the place where the Radical Reformation is being lived out. As the rural and urban poor learn to live and to work together in them, they envision and begin to develop an alternative economic order, in which the resources of a community or of a region can be used to serve the needs and interests of all, beginning with those at the bottom, and a political order, in which those formerly excluded from the exercise of public power are taking responsibility to determine their own future and are providing a foundation for a new, more participatory, democratic society. This marks them as subversives and is the reason why they are hunted down, arrested, and tortured, and sometimes killed, just as were the Anabaptists four centuries ago. But as they live this way, they challenge us as Protestants to take our own history seriously and offer us a new model of church through which we might express it. At the same time, our recovery of our Protestant identity as nonconformists could prepare us to make a significant contribution to reformation in our time.

Embracing the Cross

The Anabaptist experience of the nearness of God in the midst of suffering led them to rediscover the centrality of the cross in the life of the Christian as well as the place of the suffering servant in God's redemptive action in history. Today these same supreme realities of the gospel are being rediscovered and lived in dramatic ways by the poor, struggling for liberation, and by those identified with them in that struggle.

In my recent contacts with participants in the church of the poor in Latin America, this is what stands out as their most powerful witness, compelling me to reexamine my understanding of the gospel as well as my life of discipleship. In the midst of their suffering, the poor are surprised by the presence of God as grace, the source of new life and hope, of sharing in community, even of joy. They sense that their lives have been caught up in God's redemptive action in history. In a life-and-death struggle every day, they discover what real life in the world is all about and have a taste of the richness of the divine life as well. For them the gospel has become, once again, amazing good news.

At the same time, those who have suffered persecution and have faced death because of their faith-inspired dedication to the struggle of the poor have had a similar experience. Leonardo Boff tells of one priest in northeastern Brazil who shared the suffering of the poorest peasants and, because of it, was attacked, arrested, and tortured. He went about this work "with a joy not of this world for there is a joy that the world cannot give—the joy of suffering for the people's cause, of sharing in the passion of the Lord, and of having hammered out one more link in the chain of historical liberation being forged by God through the intermediary of human effort, for the subversion of every unjust order that stands in the way of the reign of God."[5]

Perhaps, as we Protestants reconnect with this dimension of our heritage and dare to live out our faith on the front lines of the struggle for life today, we will have a similar experience. We, too, will have a new sense of what it means to be the church as we learn how to take up the cross and share the suffering of Christ. And, in so doing,

we may be able to help those most committed to revolutionary movements of liberation to realize that they can
be faithful to their vision only as they, time and again,
turn away from the temptation to seek power and privilege and turn toward those at the bottom, in order to do
everything possible to empower them. Along this road,
the dreams and struggles of the Radical Reformers will
continue to revitalize the church and to shape history.

empowerment is the answer!

Notes

Notes

Preface

1. Daniel Schipani, ed., *Freedom and Discipleship: Liberation Theology in an Anabaptist Perspective* (Maryknoll, N. Y.: Orbis Books, 1989).

1: Luther and Liberation

1. Leonardo Boff, "Lutero entre la reforma y la liberación," *Revista Latinoamericana de Teologia* (January–April 1984): 92. Author's translation.

2. Boff, "Lutero entre la reforma y la liberación," pp. 92–93.

3. Ibid., p. 92.

4. Ibid., p. 93.

5. John Calvin, "Prefatory Address to King Francis I of France," in *Institutes of the Christian Religion,* ed. John T. McNeill, tr. Ford Lewis Battles, vol. 1 (Philadelphia: Westminster Press, 1960), p. 13.

6. Martin Luther, *A Treatise on Christian Liberty,* vol. 2 of *The Works of Martin Luther* (Philadelphia: Muhlenberg Press, 1943), p. 338.

7. Luther, *Christian Liberty,* p. 342.

8. Ibid., p. 312.

9. Martin Luther, *The Babylonian Captivity of the Church,* vol. 2 of *The Works of Martin Luther* (Philadelphia: Muhlenberg Press, 1943), p. 209.

10. Luther, *Christian Liberty,* p. 325.

11. Martin Luther, as quoted in Eugen Rosenstock-Huessy, *Out of Revolution* (New York: Four Wells, 1968), p. 449.

12. Rosenstock-Huessy, *Out of Revolution,* p. 362.

2: The Lutheran Reformation and Liberation Today

1. Martin Luther, *The Babylonian Captivity of the Church,* vol. 2 of *The Works of Martin Luther* (Philadelphia: Muhlenberg Press, 1943), p. 284.

2. Martin Luther, *A Treatise on Christian Liberty,* vol. 2 of *The Works of Martin Luther* (Philadelphia: Muhlenberg Press, 1943), p. 312.

3. Luther, *Babylonian Captivity,* p. 235.

4. Ibid., p. 241.

5. Gustavo Gutiérrez, *A Theology of Liberation* (Maryknoll, N.Y.: Orbis Books), p. 27.

6. Ibid., p. 159.

3: The Bible: Source of the Truth That Sets Us Free

1. Ulrich Zwingli, *On the Clarity and Certainty of the Word of God.*

2. John Calvin, *Institutes of the Christian Religion,* ed. John T. McNeill, tr. Ford Lewis Battle (Philadelphia: Westminster Press, 1960), I.vii.4.

3. Ibid., I.viii.3.

4. John Dillenberger and Claude Welch, *Protestant Christianity,* (New York: Charles Scribner's Sons, 1954), p. 319.

5. Calvin, *Institutes,* I.vi.2.

6. Ibid., I.vii.5.

7. Ibid., I.vii.4.

8. Ibid., I.vii.5.

9. Martin Luther, as quoted in Robert Clyde Johnson, *Authority in Protestant Christianity* (Philadelphia: Westminster Press, 1959), p. 40.

4: The Bible, the Protestant Heritage, and Liberation Today

1. Antonio Gouvêa Mendonça, "Uma Inversão Radical" (unpublished paper).

2. Ibid.

3. Pablo Richard, *La fuerza espiritual de la iglesia de los pobres* (San José, Costa Rica: Editorial DEI, 1987), p. 113.

4. Gouvêa Mendonça, "Uma Inversão Radical."

5. Robert Clyde Johnson, *Authority in Protestant Theology* (Philadelphia: Westminster Press, 1959), p. 193.

5: *Ecclesia Reformata Semper Reformanda*

1. Wilhelm Pauck, *The Heritage of the Reformation* (Glencoe, Ill.: The Free Press, 1961), p. 184.

2. John Calvin, "Prefatory Address to King Francis I of France," in *Institutes of the Christian Religion,* ed. John T. McNeill, tr. Ford Lewis Battles (Philadelphia: Westminster Press, 1960), p. 13.

3. Calvin, *Institutes,* III.vii.1.

4. Michael Walzer, *The Revolution of the Saints: A Study in the Origins of Radical Politics* (Cambridge, Mass.: Harvard University Press, 1965), p. 142.

5. Eugen Rosenstock-Huessy, *Out of Revolution* (New York: Four Wells, 1964), p. 412.

6. Calvin, "Prefatory Address," p. 12.

7. Walzer, *Revolution of the Saints,* p. vii.

6: Toward the Reinvention of the Church

1. Frederick Herzog, *God-Walk: Liberation Shaping Dogmatics* (Maryknoll, N. Y. : Orbis Books, 1988).

2. Eugen Rosenstock-Huessy, *Out of Revolution* (New York: Four Wells, 1964), pp. 38–39.

7: The Challenge of the Radical Reformers

1. Ulrich Stadler, "Cherished Instructions on Sin, Excommunication, and Community of Goods," in *Spiritual and Anabaptist Writers,* eds. George Huntston Williams and Angel M. Mergal (London: SCM Press, 1957), p. 160.

2. Thomas Münzer, "Sermon Before the Princes," in Walter Klaassen, *Anabaptism: Neither Catholic nor Protestant* (Waterloo, Ontario: Conrad Press, 1973), p.21.

3. Ibid., p. 63.

4. Sebastian Franck, "Cherished Instructions on Sin, Excommunication, and Community of Goods," in *Spiritual and Ana-*

baptist Writers, eds. George Huntston Williams and Angel M. Mergal (London: SCM Press, 1957), p. 284.

5. Stadler, "Cherished Instructions," p. 284.

6. Rutschman, "Anabaptism and Liberation Theology," p. 62.

7. Ibid., p. 63.

8. John Denck, as quoted in Rutschman, "Anabaptism and Liberation Theology," p. 62.

9. Menno Simons, "Letter to John à Lasco," in The Complete Writings of Menno Simons, ed. J. C. Wenger (Scottsdale, Pa.: Herald Press), p. 790.

10. John Hut, The Mystery of Baptism (pamphlet).

11. Howard Bender, "The Anabaptist Vision," in The Recovery of the Anabaptist Vision, ed. Guy F. Hershberger (Scottsdale, Pa.: Herald Press, 1957), p. 54.

8: Toward a Radical Reformation Today

1. Conrad Grebel in "Letters to Thomas Münzer," in Spiritual and Anabaptist Writers, eds. George Huntston Williams and Angel M. Mergal (London: SCM Press, 1957), p. 80.

2. George Blaurock, "Reminiscences of George Blaurock," in Spiritual and Anabaptist Writers, eds. George Huntston Williams and Angel M. Mergal (London: SCM Press, 1957), p. 44.

3. Grebel, "Letters to Thomas Münzer," p. 77.

4. Carlos Mesters, Defenseless Flowers (Maryknoll, N.Y.: Orbis Books, 1989), p. 5.

5. Leonardo Boff, Passion of Christ, Passion of the World (Maryknoll, N. Y.: Orbis Books, 1987), p. 120.